D0289902

LISA HARPER

A PERFECT
MESS

Why You Don't Have to Worry
About Being Good Enough for God

CEDAR RAPIDS, IOWA

WaterBrook
PRESS

A PERFECT MESS
PUBLISHED BY WATERBROOK PRESS
12265 Oracle Boulevard, Suite 200
Colorado Springs, Colorado 80921

All Scripture quotations, unless otherwise indicated, are taken from The Holy Bible, English Standard Version, copyright © 2001 by Crossway Bibles, a division of Good News Publishers. Used by permission. All rights reserved. Scripture quotations marked (MSG) are taken from The Message by Eugene H. Peterson. Copyright © 1993, 1994, 1995, 1996, 2000, 2001, 2002. Used by permission of NavPress Publishing Group. All rights reserved. Scripture quotations marked (NCV) are taken from the New Century Version®. Copyright © 1987, 1988, 1991 by Thomas Nelson Inc. Used by permission. All rights reserved. Scripture quotations marked (NIV) are taken from the Holy Bible, New International Version®. NIV®. Copyright © 1973, 1978, 1984 by International Bible Society. Used by permission of Zondervan Publishing House. All rights reserved. Scripture quotations marked (NLT) are taken from the Holy Bible, New Living Translation, copyright © 1996, 2004. Used by permission of Tyndale House Publishers Inc., Wheaton, Illinois 60189. All rights reserved.

Details in some anecdotes and stories have been changed to protect the identities of the persons involved.

ISBN 978-1-4000-7479-2
ISBN 978-0-307-45788-2 (electronic)

Copyright © 2009 by Lisa Harper

All rights reserved. No part of this book may be reproduced or transmitted in any form or by any means, electronic or mechanical, including photocopying and recording, or by any information storage and retrieval system, without permission in writing from the publisher.

Published in the United States by WaterBrook Multnomah, an imprint of the Crown Publishing Group, a division of Random House Inc., New York.

WATERBROOK and its deer colophon are registered trademarks of Random House Inc.

Library of Congress Cataloging-in-Publication Data
Harper, Lisa, 1963–
   A perfect mess : why you don't have to worry about being good enough for God / Lisa Harper. — 1st ed.
       p. cm.
   Includes bibliographical references (p.   ).
   ISBN 978-1-4000-7479-2 — ISBN 978-0-307-45788-2 (electronic)
   1. Christian women—Religious life. 2. Bible. O.T. Psalms—Criticism, interpretation, etc. I. Title.
   BV4527.H383 2009
   248.8'43—dc22
                                        2009001808

Printed in the United States of America
2010

10 9 8 7 6

SPECIAL SALES
Most WaterBrook Multnomah books are available at special quantity discounts when purchased in bulk by corporations, organizations, and special-interest groups. Custom imprinting or excerpting can also be done to fit special needs. For information, please e-mail SpecialMarkets@WaterBrookMultnomah.com or call 1-800-603-7051.

Praise for
A Perfect Mess

"No one is more solidly in our corner than God himself. He lifts us up, dusts us off, and cheers us on in the 'messy' race of life. In this delightful and often humorous journey into Psalms, Lisa Harper helps us discover God's grace in every step along the way."
— MAX LUCADO

"Lisa Harper knows life. And she knows God's Word. I love how she intertwines the two, bringing hope to the hopeless and help to everyone who's ever felt like a perfect mess. With fresh insight and poignant stories, Lisa reveals a God who brings order out of chaos with just a word…even the chaos of our lives."
— JOANNA WEAVER, author of *Having a Mary Heart in a Martha World*

"*A Perfect Mess* deftly applies the ancient truths found in Psalms to our very frazzled, contemporary lives. Don't let her breezy, easy-to-read style fool you; Lisa Harper is clearly a woman who loves the Lord and His Word, and she handles both with care, offering amusing examples from her own 'messy' life even as she encourages us to get real about our on-going need for God's cleansing grace."
— LIZ CURTIS HIGGS, best-selling author of *Bad Girls of the Bible*

"*A Perfect Mess* will cause you to breathe a sigh of relief. Finally we are assured that we aren't the only ones who need encouragement as we stare in disbelief at the chaos in our lives. Thank God for His reassuring presence, and thank God for my friend Lisa. In her own unique way, she has taken truth, stirred it with grace, and then sprinkled it with her gentle and warm writing style. The result is a delicious read that soothes the deepest parts of those of us who are a perfect mess. Read and be blessed."
— PRISCILLA SHIRER, author and Bible teacher

"This book is bursting with healing and hope. Lisa is a wonderful friend, Bible teacher, and storyteller who helps us find ourselves in Psalms and understand that just as we are, we are loved by God."

— SHEILA WALSH, Women of Faith speaker and author of *Let Go*

"I read *A Perfect Mess* from cover to cover, soaking up every word of teaching and each great story that Lisa told. She is one of my all-time favorite Bible teachers, so what a joy to learn from her in these new lessons from Psalms. I will never forget reading about Lisa's mom, who crawled underneath the bed one night to comfort her sad and hiding baby girl. What a beautiful picture of our pursuing Father's love. So grab your Bible and your favorite underlining pen, open this great book, and begin learning for yourself how our beautiful God makes something perfect and glorious from our messy lives."

— ANGELA THOMAS, best-selling author and speaker

"What do climbing trees, tight-fitting clothes, loose-fitting sweatpants, and boogie shoes have in common with the book of Psalms? Don't worry; I didn't know either, but Lisa Harper has an incredible way of exploring a text written thousands of years ago and finding the relevance to our modern lives. Lisa points out something that I already knew but was afraid to admit: we are all perfect—*messes,* that is. She reminds us that although we may be messy, our heavenly Father has big arms and doesn't mind getting dirty."

— CHONDA PIERCE, comedienne, author, and recording artist

"Lisa Harper is one of my favorite writers (and favorite people), and this is my favorite book she's ever written! I love how she connects words and connects our hearts. She makes old truths so today. I feel safe with her. I think this might be how Jesus would talk if He were walking around in our lives, in our times. I sense His presence in the middle of my mess. This book is a gift. Give it to yourself."

— LISA WHELCHEL, author of the bestseller *Creative Correction* and *The Facts of Life and Other Lessons My Father Taught Me*

A PERFECT
MESS

To my sister, Theresa Bruno,
whom I love very much.

Special thanks to my editor, Laura Barker,
whose wisdom, kindness, and wit
have kept me going throughout this book-writing venture.

CONTENTS

OUR BIGGEST AND BEST
INVISIBLE FRIEND

When I was three or four, I developed a deep and abiding relationship with a lovely middle-aged couple. I could always count on Purda and Jim to be there when I needed them, probably because they lived purely in my imagination and so were able to sync their schedules with mine. (I'm pretty sure I fashioned these make-believe pals after a sweet couple at our church named Shirley and Darryl.) The fictitious Purda was pudgy and loved to bake chocolate cupcakes, but she wasn't above shimmying up a tree with me. Jim was a steadfast nonyeller who spent his free time in the garage fixing things.

My mom was naturally a bit concerned about my penchant for inventing adult playmates. Family lore details her many attempts to dissuade me from keeping company with Purda and Jim, but I was stubbornly committed to the relationship. Poor Mom probably thought she was raising a nut job until Grandmom brought over an article from a women's magazine that claimed children with imaginary friends have above-average intelligence. Once Mom discovered that Purda and Jim might just be harbingers of academic excellence and a Mensa membership, she breathed a sigh of relief!

I don't remember exactly when I stopped frolicking with those reliable yet invisible playmates. Probably when I started kindergarten and became briefly obsessed with mastering the unicycle so I could join the circus. Much like sippy cups and "hair fountains" on the top of my head, they simply faded into the fabric of childhood. But I still think about them from time to time with fondness, because although I never actually laid eyes on Jim and his spouse, I believed with all my heart that they were in my corner. That they were *for me* no matter how many times I tracked mud into the house or forgot to use my inside voice, thereby shattering the sanctity of our home with a Tarzan-type bellow!

Maybe your pretend playmate was an invincible dragon who defended you against imaginary foes, or perhaps your childhood creativity led in a direction other than make-believe playmates. Whatever the case, I'm sure your heart still resonates with the idea of having a faithful friend who not only knows you but truly delights in you just as you are. I'm also convinced our honest longing for affection points us to a God whose love for us is unconditional. And while outgrowing imaginary friends doesn't mean our lives become any less messy (frankly I make far more mistakes at forty-five than I ever did at five), because of God's mercy, our lives can be a *perfect* mess—unquestionably tangled and blemished but when surrendered to His grace, transformed into something beautiful.

Plus, unlike my fictitious playmates, God's compassionate presence is not an illusive dream but a genuine reality, as described throughout His Word. Psalms in particular reads like a diary of God's interactions with real people with real problems in need of His gloriously real grace, which is why I'm so delighted to explore some of these passages with you.

Church father and theologian John Calvin noted that the psalms provide an "anatomy of all parts of the soul,"[1] because every emotion in the human continuum is expressed somewhere in these divine tunes. The various writers depict God to be a forever friend who doesn't ask His children to hide their "ugly" emotions. His delight in you can be felt in both grinning-from-ear-to-ear moments and drab days when you feel like life has punched you in the gut. Regardless of how well or poorly we perform, He is with us. No matter how happy or sad we feel, our heavenly Father won't walk away. Our Creator-Redeemer is always in our corner; He is absolutely and eternally *for us.*

Because there are 150 psalms, we're going to explore only a few select psalms. And since these sacred songs are not arranged chronologically in the Bible, we won't necessarily go in numerical order, but we will start with Psalm 1 and end with Psalm 150 and take a sampling of others along the way. Admittedly, this is like having to choose only a few items from a fabulous gourmet buffet. But you can be assured that every bite will be delicious. Every poetic morsel in Psalms will remind us that God's incomparable love transforms the messiness and loneliness of life into a gorgeous tapestry of grace.

Finally, while this book isn't formatted like a traditional fill-in-the-blank Bible study, my hope is that you'll find it a fresh way to engage with Scripture. Each chapter includes an icebreaker question to help you connect your own experience with the topic at hand. You'll also find personal application and reflection questions at the end of each chapter, prompting you to reflect on—and maybe discuss with a group of friends—what this all means to your life today. I will be thrilled if you select *A Perfect Mess* to discuss in your book clubs, use it for curriculum in your Sunday school class, or choose it as a guide to help your women's Bible study group to peruse Psalms.

Most of all, I sincerely pray that through this book you'll realize that no matter how many messes you've made in life, you are absolutely adored by your heavenly Father.

1

WALK THIS WAY

What Psalm 1 reveals about avoiding potholes

in the path of life

~

God's words,
creating and saving words every one,
hit us where we live.
—EUGENE H. PETERSON

I'm a sucker for fashionable shoes. Unfortunately, cool "kicks" are often synonymous with wincing in agony. Which was the case a few months ago when I became madly infatuated with a pair of black, knee-high, leather boots while shopping in Chicago. When I tried them on and pranced around in a circle to impress my friends Kim and Sharon, they both looked dubious. Kim even asked, "Are you sure they're comfortable? Because you look like you're walking funny."

I replied flippantly, "Yeah, they're comfortable. And aren't they the most gorgeous boots you've ever seen?" while intentionally taking slower steps so as not to teeter in front of them anymore.

Of course, they weren't comfortable at all. I should've done the smart thing and put those boots back into the box they came from. I should've told the solicitous Nordstrom clerk, "No thank you," and walked out of the store empty-handed. But I'm more of an impulse shopper than an intelligent consumer, especially when it comes to shoes. So I surrendered the Visa and assured myself, *They're just a little stiff because they're made of such high-quality Italian leather. It won't take long for them to get broken in, and then they'll be as comfortable as a pair of slippers.*

I foolishly decided to break them in that very night at a business event because they complemented the outfit I was wearing. I was convinced the cuteness factor far outweighed the possibility of discomfort.

Besides, I reasoned, *a little pinch is nothing compared to how hip these boots will make me look.*

Less than an hour later I was hobbling around like a geisha. And by the time the emcee introduced me, I no longer had any sensation in my toes. I limped mincingly to the podium and tried to focus on speaking while fearing my feet were in the initial stages of gangrene. All the while, my friends sat on the front row wearing "I told you so" expressions. Afterward they teased that I should've explained the new-shoe shuffle to the audience. They mused that some people might have wondered if I'd been boozing it up beforehand since I couldn't walk right all night!

> When was the last time you hobbled around in pain due to your own foolish choices?

Walking right is the theme of Psalm 1. This first song in the Psalter emphasizes how we must follow our heavenly Father's path instead of being lured off course by what ungodly people proclaim to be fashionable. And this ode to obedience includes a warning as well: attempting to be hip in ways that aren't cool with God will ultimately lead to hobbling around in pain, separated from the only One who loves you unconditionally.

"JOY" THIEVES

I can't help but grin over the fact that the book of Psalms begins with the word *happy.* And I find it especially intriguing that the happiness in Psalm 1 isn't associated with eating dark chocolate or finding a pair of designer shoes on the clearance rack. Instead this literary smiley face refers to the profound joy and satisfaction that accompany walking closely with God:[1]

> Happy are those who don't listen to the wicked,
>> who don't go where sinners go,
>> who don't do what evil people do. *Psalm 1:1, NCV*

One Sunday when I was in junior high school, I was sitting in church beside a cute lothario named Gary. You can imagine how I felt when this suave young man, who was five years older than I and the object of a huge crush on my part, put his arm around my shoulders. We were sitting a few pews in front of Dad, and although Gary's attention was so titillating I couldn't pay attention to the sermon, I could sense Dad's disapproval wafting through the sanctuary. When the service was over, my normally soft-spoken father pulled me aside and declared, "I'd better never catch you swapping slobber with that boy." Then he tersely told me to get in the car.

We drove home in uncomfortable silence, my dad staring straight ahead and me staring out the window thinking, *I hope none of my friends heard Dad. I can't believe he actually said "slobber"! Ugh, I wish he wasn't such a fuddy-duddy.* After we had pulled into the driveway and I had started walking toward the house, Dad finally broke the silence by saying, "Lisa, come over here for a minute." He motioned for me to join him by the picnic table. I approached with a cautious "Yes sir,"

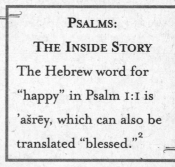

PSALMS:
THE INSIDE STORY
The Hebrew word for "happy" in Psalm 1:1 is 'ašrēy, which can also be translated "blessed."[2]

and he said, "I want you to get up on the table." I thought, *Oh man, Dad's losing it!* But he looked so serious that I obediently climbed on top of the picnic table.

Then he held up his arms and said, "Take hold of my hands. Now when I say go, I want you to try to pull me up while I try to pull you off." Of course, the minute he said go and pulled, I had to jump down because I couldn't keep my balance. Dad smiled—sort of sadly—and patted the bench beside him. When I sat down, he said, "Honey, you need to realize that it's almost impossible to raise someone else up to your standards. If you choose to be with people who have lower morals, nine times out of ten they'll pull you down to their level."

It wasn't until a year or two later, after Gary had thoroughly rebelled against his Christian upbringing and gotten a young girl pregnant, that Dad's backyard object lesson really hit home. I realized he wasn't being a fuddy-duddy when he warned me about sharing spit with the community Casanova; he was protecting me. Dad knew what my adolescent heart had yet to learn: bad company is as corrosive as battery acid. Lounging around with unrepentant rebels is a sure way to lose your joy.

> ### THE JOY OF DOING GOOD
>
> In a recent research project on the source of happiness, psychologists found that "the more virtue-building activities people engaged in, the happier they said they were both on the day in question and on the following day." But they noted with some surprise, "there was no relationship between pleasure-seeking and happiness."[3]

Which is the bottom line of the beginning of Psalm 1: happiness can't keep company with wickedness.

ABBA'S ARBORETUM

My first tour of Israel ranks way up there on the "a few of my favorite things" list. The Mount of Beatitudes left me speechless. The Wailing Wall left me in tears. And the Garden Tomb left me giddy with gratitude. But the parched terrain of the Promised Land initially left me puzzled. I guess I'd always imagined Israel as a lush green landscape dotted with fluffy white sheep and bearded guys playing harps under big shade trees (largely due to the influence of flannel-graph lessons in Vacation Bible School). It took a few days after landing at the Tel Aviv airport for me to get used to the wind-swept panorama of thornbushes, rocks, and scruffy little acacia trees. As if I were using an Etch A Sketch, I had to shake the image of a garden from my mind and twist the dials to redraw Israel as a desert.

The reality of Israel's arid topography is what makes the lush imagery in the next two verses so striking.

> They love the LORD's teachings,
>> and they think about those teachings day and night.
> They are strong, like a tree planted by a river.
>> The tree produces fruit in season,
>> and its leaves don't die.
> Everything they do will succeed. *Psalm 1:2–3, NCV*

It's unlikely this psalmist had ever seen a big tree unless it had been *transplanted,* which is a more accurate translation of the word "planted" in verse 3.[4] As a matter of fact, quality lumber was such a scarcity in Israel (except for olive trees, which are more valuable for their oil than their timber) that Solomon actually had to arrange for cedar beams to be floated in from Lebanon when they were building the temple in Jerusalem.[5] That's why this arbor metaphor is an unmistakable reference to *God's blessing;* only He could make a tree grow strong and tall in the sweltering heat and sandy soil of Israel. Only He could cultivate vegetation so perfectly that its leaves wouldn't wither in a drought.

What this means for us is that whoever has been *transplanted* into God's garden will flourish. And I really *dig* (pun intended) the psalmist's use of the term "transplanted" here, because it implies that salvation is by grace, that because we can't *plant ourselves,* God plucks us from the dark, sunless place where we'd been decaying and lovingly replants us in a perfect spot where we're guaranteed to flourish. We will get bigger and more beautiful, to the point of actually bearing fruit, as we absorb the living water our Creator provides. Plus, when our roots are anchored in Him, even figurative droughts like critical in-laws or financial crises or cancer diagnoses won't destroy us. The "leaves" of those loved by God don't die. Our heavenly Father—who also happens to have a supernatural green thumb—promises to nourish and protect His saplings.

Before we go any further, you may be wondering about the assertion that "everything they do will succeed" at the end of verse 3, which at first glance seems about as truthful as the weight listed on my driver's license until our government chose to omit that data (maybe because most people fudged on the amount). How can the psalmist label broken relationships or rebellious children or infertility or crippling depression a success? How can he sincerely sing, "Everything they do will succeed," when all of God's children experience failure of some kind or another? Has he been guzzling cough syrup, or is he just wearing overly optimistic blinders?

> **PSALMS:**
> **THE INSIDE STORY**
> Psalm 1 doesn't have a formal title or author's name, which puts it among the orphan psalms.

Neither. Because this promise of prosperity is preceded by the context "everything they do"—which in this passage is defined by spiritual obedience—"succeed" in verse 3 is in reference to walking closely with God.[6] It's essentially an Old Testament version of Romans 8:28: "And we know that for those who love God all things work together for good, for those who are called according to his purpose."

It doesn't mean we'll get everything we want exactly how and when we want it. And it sure doesn't mean everything we do will be judged successful by human standards. What it means is that ultimately our sovereign Redeemer will work *everything* out for our good and His glory because we are His people and He loves us. It means being in a real, redemptive relationship with the Creator of the universe is the true measure of success.

THE FLEETING EXISTENCE OF EVIL

God-haters, by contrast, aren't deep rooted or taken care of by a divine gardener; they're more like tumbleweeds that roll across the ground, only to inevitably disintegrate in barbed wire:

> But wicked people are not like that.
>> They are like chaff that the wind blows away.
>>> *Psalm 1:4, NCV*

I recently had oral surgery because the root of an upper molar had fractured in half, leaving me with no option but to have the tooth yanked out of my head. My dentist advised me to get an implant as opposed to an old-fashioned partial or bridge. This means that after the gaping wound from the extraction heals, the surgeon will drill a titanium screw into my jawbone, then when it grafts sufficiently, she'll affix a porcelain crown to the screw and—presto!—I'll have a shiny new molar that, according to the brochure, will last over two hundred years. (I'm not sure why the longevity of the implant is considered a selling point since the rest of me will presumably be long gone by then.)

Of course none of this six-thousand-dollar procedure is covered by insurance, and the whole process takes about a year, but I was too loopy from laughing gas to stop and think about the consequences. The worst one being that in place of my trusty old tooth, I now have a "flipper" (common dental vernacular for the fake tooth patients wear prior to getting the actual implant). Furthermore, because this flipper clips on instead of being secured with adhesive, I have a gap between it and my gum that causes me to talk with a noticeable lisp. Believe me, this is a real bummer when you gab for a living!

My dentist told me the tooth trauma actually started with a substandard root canal I had in college, which left me with a compromised chomper that probably cracked when I fell headfirst off a ladder onto a concrete floor a few years ago. He also broke the news that I'll likely need another implant in the near future. Like the hair color I was born with and the steel-trap memory I had in young adulthood, even my permanent teeth have proved to be temporary.

> **PSALMS:**
>
> **THE INSIDE STORY**
>
> In Hebrew, the book of Psalms is titled *tehillim*, which (when translated) means "songs of praise." And since each psalm was originally crafted as a song, that makes Psalms essentially the first hymnal of God's people![7]

Verse 4 explains that the wicked won't last either. Oh, they may have their season in the sun when it seems as if they're sitting on top of the world. But their days are numbered. It won't be long before God yanks those who defy Him out of their abscessed existence. Their chance of survival matches that of a snowball in the Sahara!

THEIR TRAGIC TRAIL'S END

All three of my aunts have worked in public education. One has been a middle-school teacher for decades, and the other two have taught in the classroom and also worked in administration. One of them recently told me about having to expel a high-school senior for attempting to sell prescription drugs two weeks before the end of the school year. This kid was all set to start college in the fall when he chose to become a Vicodin vendor. But my aunt didn't have the luxury of lenience, despite his status as a soon-to-be graduate. She had no choice but to call the police, because her high school has a zero-tolerance policy with regard to drugs.

When this student should have been laughing with his buddies in the locker room, he was instead being handcuffed and hauled off to jail. When he should have been striding across the stage to receive his diploma and then smiling into the camera lens of his proud papa, he was instead ostracized and alone. When he should've been listening to the lectures of university professors as a baby-faced freshman, he was instead repeating lessons from his last semester in high school. Because of very bad choices, this young man was severely punished. He was effectively barred from the life he could have enjoyed.

And so it is with the wicked. Instead of being happy and content in communion with our Creator, unrepentant sinners will ultimately be cut off from the land of the living. They will *not* pass Go, they will *not* collect two hundred dollars, and they will *not* get to graduate to glory with their classmates:

> So the wicked will not escape God's punishment.
> Sinners will not worship with God's people.
> *Psalm 1:5, NCV*

OUR CONSTANT OBSERVER

I recently had a motion-activated camera installed on my back porch by the Williamson County Sheriff's Department (chapter 7 tells the Paul Harvey part of this story). Unfortunately I didn't realize that along with the ability to capture burglars in a digital format, it also recorded me every time I opened or closed the back door. A week later one of the detectives came by to change the battery and started teasing about arresting me on animal-cruelty charges. He explained how he and several other deputies had gotten a big kick out of watching the footage of my leg stepping through a crack in the door, followed by my cat Lazarus sailing through the air like a Frisbee.

I was so embarrassed, because I love animals. But my recently adopted, houseplant-shredding tabby is a feisty little critter. Whenever I gently place Lazarus outside, he races back in before I can close the door and then attempts to shred something else before I nab him again. So I've gotten into the habit of tossing him a short distance so I can close the door without squashing any part of his anatomy in the process. (Don't worry. He always lands unharmed on his feet.) Little did I know that my

---

PSALMS: THE INSIDE STORY

The 150 individual psalms that make up the book of Psalms (also referred to as the Psalter) were written over a timespan of almost one thousand years, from Moses's era (1400 BC) until the southern Jews returned from captivity in Babylon (around 500 BC). That means these poems were penned while God's people were wandering around in the desert, when they made their bittersweet return to Jerusalem only to find the land of milk and honey had become a mess, and every season in between. It's an understatement to say the historical landscape of these lyrics is diverse; Psalms is like a comprehensive musical anthology that covers everything from Rachmaninoff to rap!

---

nightly cat toss was being viewed in living color by local law-enforcement officials. They were privy to everything; in fact, their vantage point was so intimate, they could even tell the color of my pajamas!

The next section of Psalm 1 is all about God's observation of us. In fact, the English Standard Version of the Bible puts it like this:

For the LORD knows the way of the righteous. *Psalm 1:6*

God *knows* His people. He has intimate awareness of all our ways…pet hurling and otherwise. Which makes me wonder: if we could actually see the red light of God's "camera" being activated by every thought that runs through our heads, every word that crosses our lips, and everything we do in public and private, how would we behave? Wouldn't you rather have *holy* inscribed on your divine DVD than *heinous*?

Finally, just as the sheriff-cam was bad news for the convicted criminal who used to lurk around my house, so is God's complete knowledge of human character bad news for the wicked at the end of this opening psalm:

But the wicked will be destroyed. *Psalm 1:6, NCV*

Which means that unbelievers aren't simply sitting ducks who *might* get wiped out; their annihilation is assured. God's people will be the ones hiking along the path of hope and happiness, but the wicked dudes are blithely prancing straight toward obliteration. They're going to be burned up faster than petty cash at Target!

SECURITY COMES WITH THE SHEPHERD

The guaranteed security of God's people, in contrast with the definitive destruction of those who don't follow Him, in Psalm 1 reminds me of this sermon Jesus preached in the New Testament:

When he finally arrives, blazing in beauty and all his angels with him, the Son of Man will take his place on his glorious throne.

Then all the nations will be arranged before him and he will sort the people out, much as a shepherd sorts out sheep and goats, putting sheep to his right and goats to his left.

Then the King will say to those on his right, "Enter, you who are blessed by my Father! Take what's coming to you in this kingdom. It's been ready for you since the world's foundation. And here's why:

I was hungry and you fed me,
I was thirsty and you gave me a drink,
I was homeless and you gave me a room,
I was shivering and you gave me clothes,
I was sick and you stopped to visit,
I was in prison and you came to me."

Then those "sheep" are going to say, "Master, what are you talking about? When did we ever see you hungry and feed you, thirsty and give you a drink? And when did we ever see you sick or in prison and come to you?" Then the King will say, "I'm telling the solemn truth: Whenever you did one of these things to someone overlooked or ignored, that was me—you did it to me."

Then he will turn to the "goats," the ones on his left, and say, "Get out, worthless goats! You're good for nothing but the fires of hell. And why? Because—

I was hungry and you gave me no meal,
I was thirsty and you gave me no drink,
I was homeless and you gave me no bed,

I was shivering and you gave me no clothes,
Sick and in prison, and you never visited."

Then those "goats" are going to say, "Master, what are you talking about? When did we ever see you hungry or thirsty or homeless or shivering or sick or in prison and didn't help?"

He will answer them, "I'm telling the solemn truth: Whenever you failed to do one of these things to someone who was being overlooked or ignored, that was me—you failed to do it to me."

Then those "goats" will be herded to their eternal doom, but the "sheep" to their eternal reward. *Matthew 25:31–46, MSG*

While this story portrays the "good" group as being more giving—they volunteer with Prison Fellowship and cook dinner for down-on-their-luck neighbors and share their soda with cotton-mouthed strangers—they're only emulating their Master. Because they've walked closely with Jesus, they've begun to mirror some of His mannerisms. It's not that they're inherently better than the wicked guys; sheep and goats are both stinky, hairy manure machines. (Believe it or not, I actually have a bit of first-hand experience on this issue.) Furthermore, my veterinarian friends tell me that goats are actually smarter than sheep. That means sheep don't have more intrinsic value than goats. The real reason they're elevated in this gospel imagery is their relationship with the Shepherd. He's the reason sheep get to be on the right side. He's the reason they're spared.

Just like the smelly farm animals in Matthew 25, Psalm 1 reminds us that our salvation is tied to our Shepherd. Without Him, we would surely follow a delinquent gang of goats down the path of destruction. But God's perfect grace blazes a trail of hope and happiness for messy people like us.

When we follow our Father's directions, we'll be able to "walk right," even when teetering on a pair of ill-fitting, too-cool-for-school boots!

⇒ *The right-now relevance of Psalm 1* ⇒

God's love frees us to steer clear of the path of destruction and keep step with Him in joyful obedience.

ENOUGH ABOUT ME. WHAT ABOUT YOU?

1. It's been said that the primary purpose of biblical poetry (like that of Psalms) is not so much to *teach* us as to *reach* us. What kind of poetry or song lyrics do you emotionally resonate with the most?

2. Reread Psalm 1:1. List the top five people you're most likely to listen to when you need advice. Do you typically walk away happy after listening to their counsel? Why or why not?

3. Describe a situation in which you were metaphorically "pulled off the picnic table" as a result of hanging around with ungodly rebels.

4. Read Jeremiah 17:7–8 and Matthew 5:3–12. How are the common themes in these passages connected to the overall theme of Psalm 1?

5. Compare Psalm 1:4 with Luke 3:15–17. Why do you think God "winnows" wicked people from His followers? Have you ever felt the need to separate yourself from some people because of their cruddy attitude about our Creator-Redeemer? How did you make the break?

6. What movie or book can you think of that reflects the theme of Psalm 1? Explain the parallels you see.

2

LEAPING OVER LEGALISM

What Psalm 62 says about wriggling out

of the trap of wrong expectations

Our Lord God must be a pious man
to be able to love rascals.
I cannot do it, and yet I am a rascal myself.
—MARTIN LUTHER

When I was nine years old, I got busted by Fran, a neighbor with a towering beehive hairdo. Let me assure you that Fran was not an unkind person. She was nothing like Peggy Brooks's grandmother, who chased neighborhood kids with a broom if we attempted to "trespass" through her yard while playing freeze-tag or hide-and-seek. Fran was actually one of my favorite adults on Valencia Avenue. She dressed in tight, colorful clothes that resembled the outfits Cher wore on *The Sonny and Cher Show,* albeit without the cutouts, which would've been pretty scary, considering Fran's big-boned frame. Plus, the macramé plant hangers cradling spider ferns in her living room gave me the impression that she had been a cool hippie before becoming a middle-aged suburbanite with a colossal coiffure.

So when Fran clomped across her backyard and pounded on our front door, she wasn't being cruel or persnickety. She was simply concerned about my well-being after inadvertently witnessing me leap across her horizon. There she was on her deck, enjoying the sunset while sipping a vodka martini (we were a largely Baptist neighborhood, and Fran's social drinking made her appear even more wildly exotic), when she looked up and saw me race across the gables and launch myself into the air, jumping the gap between our house and the detached garage. The leap was a long time ago, but I like to think I appeared graceful and gazelle-like.

Unfortunately, I didn't know I had an audience until I heard Fran exhale an expletive after I landed on the opposite roof.

I guess her alarm was justified, because the space between rooftops was about twelve feet. If I hadn't aimed for the lower pitch of the garage roof, thereby gaining some distance, I would have plummeted to the concrete patio. Things could've gotten ugly.

I don't recall what was going through my head when I took that leap. Maybe I was Batgirl escaping from the Joker. Or maybe I was reenacting my favorite circus trapeze act. All I know is that our laid-back neighborhood hippie transformed into a woman on a mission after observing my fortunate landing. She plunked down her beverage, got out of her chair, and headed straight for our front door. And I knew I was about to be in big trouble!

> Did you tend to be more of a rule follower or a rule bender in your youth? How about now? Would your friends describe you as typically compliant or more of a rebel at heart?

While I wasn't often outed by the neighborhood watch, daredevil behavior played an integral role in my childhood. A typical summer day involved hurling myself off roofs, trees, and high dives. And racing horses, dirt bikes, and skateboards. And crashing into barns, ditches, and barbed wire! Much to my big sister's chagrin, I preferred to climb trees than sit under them and have a tea party. I could not have cared less about watching the Miss America pageant, but my eyes were riveted to the television when Evel Knievel attempted to jump his motorcycle across the Snake River Canyon in Idaho.

My rascally behavior conflicted greatly with the ideals of my small, conservative, Southern town, where external conformity was preached from the pulpit and practiced in most homes. My earliest memories include a repressive list of dos and don'ts:

- Good girls always help the teacher clean up after class.
- Good girls don't talk back to adults.
- Good girls wear dresses to church (preferably with black patent leather shoes in the winter and white sandals in the summer).
- Good girls memorize Bible verses.
- Good girls don't dance or wiggle anything.
- Good girls use their inside voices even when they're outside.
- Good girls don't play cards or go to movies unless the flicks are animated (although Disney films were still questionable because of all that trashy magic and sorcery).
- Good girls always behave the way others expect them to.

A Porsche's worth of dollars spent in therapy has enlightened me to the fact that risking life and limb was a way of rebelling against the kill-joy culture of my childhood. It was an adolescent attempt to be honest and free, to wriggle out of the hypocritical confines of conservatism masquerading as Christianity. I might be forced to wear tights and to whisper in Sunday school, but, doggone it, I was going to wear cutoffs and bellow like Tarzan during the week!

HAPPY FACES AND HOSIERY DON'T EQUAL HOLINESS

My craving for candor is one of the main reasons I gravitate toward the psalms; I love their *Sitz im Leben* style. "Sitz im Leben" is the German phrase that describes the "real life" setting of the psalms. Much like country music songs that describe a couple in love or a woman celebrating the fact that she got her undies on sale at Wal-Mart or some guy crying in his beer because his hound dog got run over, these biblical lyrics deal with the less-than-lovely stuff that happens to regular folks. They aren't full of pithy, positive sentiments or sugarcoated with false hope.

PSALMS: THE INSIDE STORY

The psalms are typically classified into several categories, including but not limited to:

- *wisdom* psalms
- *penitential* psalms
- royal or *Messianic* psalms
- *thanksgiving* psalms
- *imprecatory* psalms
- psalms of *ascent* or pilgrimage
- psalms of *lament*

Although Bible scholars don't always agree on how to categorize a psalm,[1] we do know these songs were written by numerous songwriters. While nearly half are attributed to David, other lyricists include his son Solomon, Asaph (David's "worship leader"), the sons of Korah, Moses, and some guy named Ethan. Plus, a few are officially listed as anonymous (often referred to as the orphan psalms).[2]

More important, the psalms remind us to trust in God's power, not our own puny attempts to live righteously. Consider the opening words of Psalm 62, written by King David:

> For God alone my soul waits in silence;
> from him comes my salvation. *Psalm 62:1*

In other words, wearing a happy face and hose to church doesn't make us good girls any more than painting racing stripes on a Yugo makes it a sports car. Walking in faith means trusting in God alone, not in what we say or do or wear. It means being honest about the fact that each of us is a mess and we need God's mercy. It means recognizing our complete dependence on His protection, provision, and providence.

German pastor, writer, and theologian Dietrich Bonhoeffer once preached an entire sermon on this single verse. One of his main points was how uncomfortable most humans are with stillness…with waiting.[3] Boy, do I get that! All too often I try to choreograph life. Instead of waiting on God to do His thing, I attempt to manipulate the details on my own.

Frankly, I think fixating on our own competency—or obsessing over our incompetency—is one of the biggest mistakes believers make. Because when we focus all our energy on trying to be in control, we forget our innate sinfulness and our desperate need for God. We succumb to *moralism,* the false belief that somewhere in our hearts resides the aptitude for perfection and the ability to fix everything that's wrong with our world. Then we jump on

WHAT THE LADY KNOWS

According to *The Lady's Guide to Perfect Gentility,* just a few of the bad habits every woman should avoid at all costs include:

- to look steadily at anyone;
- to cross her legs;
- to remain without gloves;
- to fold carefully her shawl, instead of throwing it with graceful negligence upon a table;
- to laugh immoderately;
- to beat time with her feet and hands.[4]

I don't know about you, but this list is enough to prompt yours truly to give a decidedly unladylike whoop of joy, knowing that nothing on this etiquette list or any other will affect God's view of us!

the hamster wheel of working increasingly harder to be both holy and in control until we can't imagine living one more day under the tyranny of "need tos" and "shoulds."

The depressing reality of Christians' working so hard to pretend that we have our lives totally together—and therefore should be in charge of everybody else's—makes me want to say bad words and gobble chocolate. But there is hope beyond cussing and carbohydrates. There is a path that veers away from the exhausting effort of self-reliance and back to the security we have in divine redemption.

And we'll find the trailhead when we take our eyes off ourselves and instead focus on *who God is.*

GRAB A PIECE OF THE ROCK

> He only is my rock and my salvation,
>   my fortress; I shall not be greatly shaken.
> *Psalm 62:2*

Using the petite adverb *only,* David points us to the sole source of our security and highlights the peace that comes with theocentric, or God-centered, living. New Testament scholar Herman Ridderbos elaborated on this concept by noting how two different types of Bible passages— "indicative" and "imperative"—work together in showing us how to "do life" God's way. (These terms also describe the grammatical moods of the Greek language, the original language of most of the New Testament.)[5] The *indicatives* are a declaration of *who God is,* while the *imperatives* refer to *how Christians should live* in response to God.

And much like chubby women should always wear one-piece bathing suits, the imperatives (how we live) should always be encased and inspired by the indicatives (who God is). In other words, all our attempts to behave like good Christian women are meaningless unless we really know whom we're behaving for.

In Psalm 62:2, the indicative truth is that God is our rock and salvation, and the imperative challenge is to "not be greatly shaken." David's not suggesting that we pull ourselves up by our bootstraps and tough it out; he's saying that *if* we put our confidence in God, *then* we'll be able to stand firm in the storms of life. *If* we rest in God's worthiness, *then* we'll be like those Weebles toys: we might wobble, but we won't fall down!

WHEN *FAMILY FEUD* IS THE ONLY SHOW PLAYING

But now David's tone segues from committed disciple to weary daddy:

> How long will all of you attack a man
>> to batter him,
>> like a leaning wall, a tottering fence?
> They only plan to thrust him down from his high position.
>> They take pleasure in falsehood.
> They bless with their mouths,
>> but inwardly they curse.   *Selah.*
>> *Psalm 62:3–4*

I've spent the last several weeks listening to polished politicians give speeches at both the Democratic and Republication national conventions. And I've noticed that much of the rhetoric includes statements about the American family. It's been implied that *family* equals peace and happiness, that *family* leads to good fortune. I can't help but think, *Not for everyone. What about people who come from irreparably broken families? What about the children of parents who hit hard after drinking heavily? What about spouses who've been betrayed and abandoned?*

While God designed the family to be a place where we find peace and joy, because we live in a fallen world, the family can still be fantastically flawed. Some people's family of origin is more like competing on *Survivor* than living with the Waltons. Even intact, harmonious families aren't perfect, and the people we love most will let us down. Just like us, they're fallible.

King David certainly experienced that. As a matter of fact, many scholars believe David's betrayal by his son Absalom[6] is the setting for this psalm and that painful treachery is the underlying theme of verses 3 and 4. Can you imagine the stabbing pain in David's heart as he wrote about his son's disloyalty and pending failure? How sad it was for him to sing about his little boy who'd become a duplicitous man? Yet he still punctuated this mournful melody with the word *Selah,* an expression that provides a momentary pause to weigh what was just said (or sung). That one little word—*selah*—reveals David was earnestly focusing on God's message in the midst of personal crisis. While he must have been blindsided by Absalom's deceit, David did not lose sight of God's faithfulness.

I think the disappointed-parent perspective in Psalm 62 is very important because our culture tends to view moms and dads through the lens of their children's behavior. Which doesn't sound so bad so long as your offspring is Mother Teresa or Billy Graham! But as most parents will admit, even good kids have really bad days. Or years.

My friend Kathy has a precious little boy who recently morphed into a pit bull and has started biting his classmates. As you can imagine, his untoward teething isn't well received by the other mommies. Consequently, Kathy feels like a pariah in the preschool parking lot. It's bad enough to have others judge us for our own messes; what a bummer to be blamed for our kids' mistakes!

Fortunately, David's attitude here reminds parents they can trust in God's unwavering affection, even when their progeny throw tantrums in the grocery store, pulverize the neighbor's roses, or emulate vampires.

I Know That I Know That I Know

Now I imagine David gently placing the picture of Absalom back on the mantel with a heavy sigh and picking up his guitar to continue this song:

> For God alone, O my soul, wait in silence,
>> for my hope is from him.
> He only is my rock and my salvation,
>> my fortress; I shall not be shaken. *Psalm 62:5–6*

Notice that David shifts his thinking from "I shall not be greatly shaken" in verse 2 to "I shall not be shaken" at the end of verse 6. It's as if David earlier left open the door of doubt—just a crack—by saying he wouldn't be greatly shaken, but now he's slamming it shut by declaring that he won't be shaken at all. The sentiment coursing through these verses is "No way, baby! I'm not going anywhere as long as I'm safe inside the fortress of the Almighty!"

You can be sure David didn't slip away and listen to some motivational tapes and determine to overcome his adversity by setting achievable goals. And he wasn't suddenly infused with energy because he stayed at a Holiday Inn Express. No, David's still the same mistake-prone man he was when he started this psalm. In fact, the slight mood swing from verse 2 to verse 6 reflects the genuine wrestling of a regular guy, not the fake piety of someone pretending to be perfect. David isn't playing the part of a big hero here; the Holy Spirit just reminded him of how huge his God is!

Perfectly Large and in Charge

One of my typically tasteful girlfriends uses the redneck metaphor "it's like two ticks with no dog" to describe what happens when individuals try to get all their needs met by another person. David touches on the same theme, albeit without the colorful colloquialism, in the second half of Psalm 62:

> On God rests my salvation and my glory;
>> my mighty rock, my refuge is God.
>
> Trust in him at all times, O people;
>> pour out your heart before him;
>> God is a refuge for us.   *Selah*
>
> Those of low estate are but a breath;
>> those of high estate are a delusion;
> in the balances they go up;
>> they are together lighter than a breath. *Psalm 62:7–9*

After affirming God's worthiness in verse 7 and beseeching everyone to trust Him in verse 8, David proclaims that regardless of how much wealth or power people have—whether they live in a mansion with a plasma television in every room and a butler with a British accent guarding the front door (high estate) or in a government-subsidized apartment with holes in the dry wall and a collection agent knocking on the front door (low estate)—no one but God deserves our absolute devotion. Whether prosperous or poor, human beings aren't worthy of worship. If we put our hope solely in humanity, we're going to need a whole lot of Prozac!

The same holds true, David observes, of trusting in material wealth:

> Put no trust in extortion;
>> set no vain hopes on robbery;
>> if riches increase, set not your heart on them.

Once God has spoken;

> twice have I heard this:

that power belongs to God,

> and that to you, O Lord, belongs steadfast love.

For you will render to a man

> according to his work. *Psalm 62:10–12*

I know, I know. At first glance the tail end of this tune sounds as if David is reversing himself and suggesting that God takes care of us only when we earn a perfect score on our Good Girl report cards. It's one of those "Say what?" passages that cause even the most dutiful Bible-study chick to pause in confusion while holding a yellow highlighter aloft over her homework! But despite the flavor of our English translations, the original language of the phrase "render to a man according to his work" doesn't actually mean "God gives better stuff to folks who work their fannies off!" In fact the word *render* (the NIV translates this as *reward*) comes from the Hebrew root word *šālēm,* which means "being at peace or being fulfilled."[7] So David's point isn't so much about the virtues of a strong work ethic as it is about the worthiness of our heavenly Father. Unlike human leaders, the Lord can be trusted to be absolutely true in His dealings with us. His throne will never be compromised by dishonesty or duplicity. He will never shortchange us to benefit Himself. God is and will always be the perfect Ruler.

If any psalm deserves the title "It's Not About Us; It's All About God," it's this one!

GOD BLESS THIS MESS!

I really wish my well-intentioned childhood pastors had emphasized the promises about freedom in Scripture more than their opinions about drinking and dancing. I wish I hadn't felt the pressure to wear a "good girl" mask for so much of my life. I wish I'd winked at a few more grouchy deacons and embraced a few more church visitors who reeked of cigarette smoke. Even now I occasionally find myself wearing that tattered old mask…like when I won't venture outside before noon on Sunday—even though I attended worship services on Saturday night—for fear that someone driving by might think I'm a reprobate. Or when I judge someone else to be less spiritually mature because I spotted her texting on her cell phone during Bible study.

Maybe you've worn a similar mask. Maybe you've felt pressured by the "shoulds" and "need tos" of rule-based religiosity. Maybe you've based your critique of others on whether or not they jumped through the same hypocritical hoops you did. Perhaps you've harbored dreams of roaring up to church on a Harley or wearing a dress that reveals the butterfly tattoo on your shoulder.

Thankfully it's never too late to unwrap God's lavish gift of liberty. To live and love in response to His amazing grace. To revel in our own redemption story. To jump off the hamster wheel of morality and rest in the mercy of our Creator. Besides, don't you think a few more unconventional Christians would make our world a much nicer place to be?

The right-now relevance of Psalm 62

God's love frees us from meaningless rules and religious propriety, which means we can live authentically and abundantly by relying on Him instead of ourselves.

ENOUGH ABOUT ME. WHAT ABOUT YOU?

1. Read Hebrews 12:1. What rules, spoken or unspoken, have marked your past experience at church or with Christians? (I'm referring to religious rules as opposed to biblical boundaries like the Ten Commandments, which God designed for our protection and well-being.) Which of these religious rules have felt the most stifling or burdensome to you personally? What are some practical ways you could wriggle out from under those unhealthy regulations?

2. Why do you think organized religion has historically squelched individual liberty? How does that measure up with what you read in Galatians 5:1–6?

3. In light of David's words about finding rest in God alone in Psalm 62, describe a recent time when you felt completely safe and sound in God's care.

4. While we usually think we know better than to trust in superficial things like wealth and power, what are some other inappropriate things or people by which we tend to measure our worth
   and security?

5. Reread Psalm 62:1–2, 5–6. Why do you think David emphasized waiting in silence? What percentage of your prayer life is
   reserved for listening instead of talking? Describe a recent selah
   moment, a time when you literally paused while praying or
   reading the Bible because you wanted to weigh what you'd just
   heard.

6. Read Psalm 46. In verse 5 we find the same language of not
   being moved that we read in Psalm 62:6, this time with regard
   to a holy city. What do you think a modern city of resolute,
   unwavering God-followers would look like? Have you ever seen
   or experienced a faithful community where everyone feels wel-
   come to be authentic and checklists for "good girl" behavior are
   figuratively turned into origami?

3

TUMBLING TOWARD APPROVAL

How Psalm 139 describes the way

God sees the beauty behind our blemishes

Unfortunately, often our faith doesn't penetrate
to our unfavorable feelings about ourselves.
—MARVA DAWN

Throughout childhood, two of my closest friends were Ginny Bishop and Brenda Brown. Brenda was also my second cousin, so I suppose our moms would've forced the relationship on us whether we liked it or not. But we really did like each other. And Ginny was one of five sisters, so being a good girlfriend was second nature to her. From the glitter-and-glue days of elementary school through the rapture and rupture of high school, the three of us remained an invincible, inseparable team. Not unlike the cool cats on *The Mod Squad* or the gorgeous heroines of *Charlie's Angels*…at least that's how we imagined it!

My favorite memories from our triune kinship center on the mock Olympic gymnastic competitions we frequently staged in Ginny's front yard. Ginny would pop one of her parents' classical music tapes into a boom box, then the contest would officially begin with as much pomp and circumstance as we could manage with whatever household items we scrounged up. We especially liked dancing around with the multicolored scarves that served as the flags of whatever fictional countries each of us represented. After the stirring opening ceremonies, we made a corporate decision regarding the sequence of our presentations. Then we each took a turn performing an extemporaneous routine for the other two to judge.

It should probably be noted that, while all three of us were athletically inclined, none of us had ever taken gymnastics lessons. So, much like the auditions of certain tone-deaf contestants on *American Idol,* our performances were infused with great enthusiasm but were a bit sketchy on the technical side. Still, I like to think that our lack of formal training propelled us to new artistic heights. For example, since I never quite mastered the compulsory back handspring, I often used the Japanese plum tree at the edge of the lawn as a prop. I reasoned that incorporating a few graceful swings from its lower branches should earn big points for creativity.

I can't help but smile when thinking about our final competition after years of hurling our bodies about in what we convinced ourselves were routines any Olympian gymnast would be proud to call her own. Having come to the realization that none of our other high-school friends spent hours rolling around in the grass for grins, we finally agreed that it was time to hang up our ratty leotards for good. But we wanted to go out with a dramatic flourish, so we began dreaming up one last glorious event. We planned our swan song for weeks, taking care to make sure our routines were flawless and our outfits as tacky as possible.

When the appointed afternoon arrived, Ginny blasted the Bach a bit louder than usual, and we paraded across her yard with more panache than ever for the opening ceremonies. Cars literally began to slow down in order to watch the spectacle! I think their curiosity was partly fueled by the fact that Ginny's house was conveniently located on a scenic boulevard where drivers tended to poke along, admiring the stately old homes. Most of them probably assumed that our sporting melodrama was something the neighborhood association had sponsored for their entertainment, like an outdoor concert or a chili cookoff. However, they did seem to sense this particular show was the end of an era, because as the contest wore on, a few drivers pulled over to the edge of the road and began to honk their horns and yell support out their windows.

Unfortunately, I found it much easier to gain the appreciation of passersby than to earn points from Brenda and Ginny, who prided themselves on being strict judges. In fact, despite my best efforts, despite the blood, sweat, and tears spilled in homage to grass gymnastics, despite my impeccable execution of both a trapezelike plum tree move and the compulsory cartwheel handstand, I still didn't score a perfect ten. Instead I closed out my tumbling career with a humble seven and a half!

> In what specific arenas do you feel like you never quite measure up to other people's expectations?

While my juvenile foray into front-yard gymnastics resulted in just a few minor scars on my shins, performing before the altar of human approval in my twenties and thirties yielded much more serious wounds. Whenever I heard disappointment or disapproval voiced in my direction, I felt as if a big *W* for *worthless* was painted across my chest. If someone gave me a low score as a friend, teammate, co-worker, or Bible teacher, I didn't chalk it up to subjective preference. I considered it a personal failure. Like Pavlov's puppy, I learned to crave clapping because I associated applause with value and affection. So I jumped higher and harder, hoping to earn favor from my judges.

Maybe you too have exhausted yourself striving to be sweeter or thinner or a better scrapbooker. Perhaps you've crafted Bible study answers with the goal of impressing the girls in your small group. It's easy to fall prey to the feel-good addiction of other people's approval.

But life-by-scorecard is exhausting. Judges change. Rules change. Venues change. Which means that even if we're named Most Valuable Player one day, our name might be flashing in neon on the JumboTron as "the loser" the next. The very same people who lauded us as heroes in the past might voice insults in the future. Human approval is a fickle goddess. Sometimes she'll embrace you, and sometimes she'll eviscerate you. Eventually she'll inflict so much emotional damage that you'll doubt whether you're worthy of taking up space on this planet, much less strutting your stuff across the lawn of life.

Sadly, after twenty years in vocational ministry, I've realized that many of us are just as prone to perform for God as for anyone else. You've probably noticed people putting on their best behavior at church—or perhaps caught yourself doing the same thing. Like kids playing dress-up, we pretend to be glossier versions of ourselves, as if we're afraid we won't make it into "God's club" unless we put on a good show.

FROM BLOOPER REELS TO BEST IN SHOW

On those days—or weeks!—when we feel like we don't measure up, like our lives are one long blooper reel, we can find hope in what King David wrote in Psalm 139:

> O LORD, you have searched me
> and you know me. *Psalm 139:1, NIV*

My counselor said the yearning she hears people repeat over and over again in her office is "I just want someone to know me." That's certainly the running theme of my sessions with her—my deep longing for intimacy, to be totally understood and truly loved. Which is why I treasure the opening lines of Psalm 139. They whisper the miraculous truth that God *gets me*. The Creator of the universe is familiar with every single nook and cranny in my crooked heart and soul!

> You know when I sit and when I rise;
> you perceive my thoughts from afar.

You discern my going out and my lying down;
>   you are familiar with all my ways.
Before a word is on my tongue
>   you know it completely, O LORD. *Psalm 139:2–4, NIV*

Of course, I didn't always find these lines reassuring. I used to think that, along with trying to impress others, I had to try to win God over with a "good girl" routine. And because my behavior is so often flawed—sometimes laughably abysmal—I assumed He was sitting on a golden throne of judgment, looking down at me with pursed lips and holding a red pen. Surely God shook His big, holy head in disapproval of my shortcomings a gazillion times a day. Surely He scratched a big F by my name each time my file came up for review. My glaring imperfections caused me to doubt that a perfect God could ever really accept a defective girl like me. I felt sure the only reason I'd get to squeak in heaven's door was because Jesus felt sorry for me and talked His Father into it. Although I walked down an aisle to confess my sins and my need for Christ's love and forgiveness when I was seven, it took decades longer to believe that Jesus actually likes me, that He doesn't merely *deliver* me but wholeheartedly *delights* in me.

AIN'T NO MOUNTAIN HIGH ENOUGH

The idea of God's enclosing us in His hands can be taken two ways, depending on our spiritual posture. When we're in rebellion and running away from God, being hemmed in can feel restrictive. But when we're in communion with our Creator, His fencing promotes a feeling of security and well-being, which is what David describes in the following verses:

You hem me in—behind and before;
> you have laid your hand upon me.
Such knowledge is too wonderful for me,
> too lofty for me to attain.

Where can I go from your Spirit?
> Where can I flee from your presence?
If I go up to the heavens, you are there;
> if I make my bed in the depths,
>> you are there.
> *Psalm 139:5–8, NIV*

When I was five years old, my mom and dad divorced. Unlike the idealistic splits depicted on television, theirs was ugly. And like many children from divorced families, I thought it was partly my fault. I thought I must have done something wrong. If only I'd been a better little girl—if I had been sweeter or kinder or used my inside voice more often—maybe Dad wouldn't have left. So I resolved to be so good that nothing that bad could ever happen again. I was determined to make straight A's and to act nice and to never let Mom see me sad, because, goodness knows, she didn't need any more grief.

One day not long after the divorce was final, the pressure of being perfect got to be too much. Deeply upset, I crawled under my bed so I could cry alone. As I was finally letting out all that emotion, I heard Mom calling me for dinner. But I didn't answer, because I couldn't control my tears—and I thought good girls weren't supposed to cry. Soon I heard her footsteps padding down the hall. When she paused in my doorway, I held my breath, hoping she'd leave. Instead she asked gently, "Lisa, honey, are you under the bed?"

Finally I murmured, "Yes ma'am." I lay there in utter misery, ashamed of my failure and certain I was about to get into trouble. Then the dust ruffle lifted, and my mom's concerned face appeared. Without another word Mom got down on the floor, wedged herself under the bed, and lay down right next to me.

That's the image that comes to my mind when I ponder God's omnipresence as described in Psalm 139:7–12. On our worst days, when we're trying to hide our misery or conceal our failures, our perfect God doesn't stand at a distance, waiting for us to pull ourselves together. He crawls right in beside us, amid the dust bunnies and clutter of our lives, to show that we're never alone in our messes. In fact, that's the very reason Jesus left the shiny halls of heaven to dine in the dusty homes of ordinary people: because God refuses to leave us alone to wallow in our misery and sin.

> If I rise on the wings of the dawn,
> > if I settle on the far side of the sea,
> even there your hand will guide me,
> > your right hand will hold me fast.
>
> If I say, "Surely the darkness will hide me
> > and the light become night around me,"
> even the darkness will not be dark to you;
> > the night will shine like the day,
> > for darkness is as light to you.
> > *Psalm 139:9–12, NIV*

No matter where we go, no matter what we do, God is *with us*. His holy hands won't let go of us.

BEAUTY IS IN THE EYE OF OUR BEHOLDER

Although the next few verses may sound like a narcissist admiring his own buff physique, this really isn't about David's being preoccupied with his reflection in the mirror.

> For you created my inmost being;
>> you knit me together in my mother's womb.
> I praise you because I am fearfully and wonderfully made;
>> your works are wonderful,
>> I know that full well. *Psalm 139:13–14, NIV*

Rather than admiring himself, David is celebrating God as his Creator, and in that context he's reveling in the fact that *God don't make junk!* The awesome right-now application of this passage is that you and I can rest in God's great affection—even on those days when we're tempted to cut people off in traffic, when our fat jeans are too tight, and when it looks like we're in last place on this world's scoreboard—because He views us through rose-colored glasses, tinted by the blood of Jesus.

> My frame was not hidden from you
>> when I was made in the secret place.
> When I was woven together in the depths of the earth,
>> your eyes saw my unformed body.
> All the days ordained for me
>> were written in your book
>> before one of them came to be. *Psalm 139:15–16, NIV*

Before your biological dad ever made the first pass at your birth mom, God knew there would be a you. He planned your first breath long before your mama's obstetrician smacked you on your bare bottom. God fashioned every cell, sculpted each bone, and painted the color of your eyes and skin. Then He stepped back and said, "Isn't she lovely?"

One morning recently I looked in the mirror and was mortified to realize that what I initially thought were sheet creases around my mouth were actually permanent lines. As I walk wincingly into middle age, it does my heart good to remember that God planned every moment of our lives. Better yet, He thinks you and I are wonderful—wrinkles or not!

> ### PSALMS:
> ### THE INSIDE STORY
> "All the days" in verse 16 has a second meaning when viewed through the progressive revelation of the New Testament, because by trusting in Jesus as our Savior, we're assured of living forever with God in heaven. That means all our days won't stop with bodily death. Our story won't end with a tombstone and a flattering epitaph. A Christian's days actually continue into eternity![1]

> How precious to me are your thoughts, O God!
> How vast is the sum of them!
> Were I to count them,
> they would outnumber the grains of sand.
> When I awake,
> I am still with you. *Psalm 139:17–18, NIV*

As David segues from God's knowledge *about David's thoughts* (verses 2–4) to God's *thoughts about David,* he reaches for an image of something incalculable. I mean, really, have you ever tried to count sand? The number of grains in even a small handful would take all day to calculate, so just imagine trying to add up every itty-bitty grain from all the seashores, lakesides, and river bottoms in the world. Even Dustin Hoffman's *Rain Man* couldn't accomplish that counting feat! David's gritty comparison alludes to the fact that God thinks about us constantly. We are always on His mind.

DAVID THROWS A CURVE

As we consider God's constant thoughts toward us, it prompts the question: how much of our own thought life revolves around Him? David certainly has strong words for those who *don't* have room for God in their itty-bitty brains!

> If only you would slay the wicked, O God!
>> Away from me, you bloodthirsty men!
> They speak of you with evil intent;
>> your adversaries misuse your name.
> Do I not hate those who hate you, O LORD,
>> and abhor those who rise up against you?
> I have nothing but hatred for them;
>> I count them my enemies. *Psalm 139:19–22, NIV*

Remember how John Calvin described Psalms as an "anatomy of all parts of the soul"? This seemingly abrupt transition in Psalm 139 reveals David's utter disdain for the enemies of God. When he remembers the wicked, he gets red in the face and blurts out his bad feelings. He simply can't stand those God-hating jerks!

I'm so glad David didn't feel the need to whitewash his indignation before bringing it before the Lord. We'll explore more "peeved passages" like this in chapter 6, but suffice it to say that mad isn't always bad in

CEDAR RAPIDS, IOWA

Scripture. God doesn't expect us to play nice with evil people. You would defend your best girlfriend if you heard someone slandering her. How much more should we defend our heavenly Father? Not for His sake—God can fry adversaries into grease spots anytime He wants—but because it's the right thing to do when you love Him.

However, even though he's just expressed rage about ungodly people, David isn't screaming from some better-than-thou throne of self-righteousness. He isn't slinging critical stones from a glass house. David knows full well that he is capable of cruddy stuff too. So he asks God for help.

> ### GOD IS IN THE DETAILS
>
> In reminding the disciples to trust God to care for them, Jesus noted, "Even the hairs of your head are all numbered" (Luke 12:7). Scientists tell us that, on average, each person's head carries about 100,000 hair follicles, with some particularly thick-haired people having as many as 150,000.[2] So if God knows how many hairs relocated from your scalp to your brush this morning, you can be sure He also knows what thoughts are cluttering your mind today.

> Search me, O God, and know my heart;
>> test me and know my anxious thoughts.
> See if there is any offensive way in me,
>> and lead me in the way everlasting.
> *Psalm 139:23–24, NIV*

I love that this psalm ends with David's baring his heart before the Lord and asking God to remove anything that offends Him. *See if there is any offensive gunk in my heart and guide me, Father.*

What a beautiful request for us to pray even today. Because of divine grace, we don't have to *perform* for God, yet we should still have the desire to *please* Him. And what better way to please our Creator than by humbly asking Him to have His way in our lives?

THE "WOWED BY GOD" WIGGLES

Sometimes when I'm pondering what a miracle it is for God to gaze at me through the lens of Jesus and use words like *beautiful* and *wonderful* to describe me, I like to imagine what it will be like when I actually get to see Him face to face—when I finish this stumbling, all-too-human routine and stand before all that is sacred, hoping the Alpha and Omega didn't notice my one-footed landings or cellulite. I picture myself watching in open-mouthed wonder as He

> ### PSALMS:
> ### THE INSIDE STORY
> The Hebrew word for heart— *lēbāb*—can be difficult to translate because it doesn't typically refer to a physical human heart. Instead it refers to the core of one's being: our thought life, emotions, and understanding.[3]

stands up, wearing a sweatshirt that says, "I'm her Dad!" and cheers with reckless abandon, all the while holding high a card emblazoned with the number ten.

That vision is almost enough to propel my over-forty self outside to turn cartwheels again! How about you? How does having God as your biggest fan make you feel?

The youngest son of my friend Kim has listened to her loving affirmations so many times that he completely believes them. Just the other day I was at their house, and Kim said to him, "Honey, you're the cutest boy in the world."

Benji replied, "I know, Mommy. Now will you help me with my math homework?"

I sat there bemused by what initially sounded like an eleven-year-old's overconfidence, but then it dawned on me: *that's how God wants us to totally trust in His love.* Believing we are adored by our Abba isn't self-congratulatory or cocky; it just means we've stopped tumbling for God's approval and are instead thoroughly enjoying our undeserved, preferential treatment. It means His perfect grace has finally conquered our self-hatred.

So now we can flip head over heels for sheer joy!

The right-now relevance of Psalm 139

God's love frees us from performing so we can relax and rejoice with the assurance that He knows us completely and adores us just as we are.

ENOUGH ABOUT ME. WHAT ABOUT YOU?

1. Whose approval here on earth have you danced the hardest for? Why do you think that person's opinion matters so much to you?

2. Which of your gifts and abilities are most likely to be acknowledged by others? Which ones are most likely to be overlooked?

3. Read all of Psalm 139. Which phrases do you identify with the most right now, and why? Which verses do you have a hard time applying to yourself?

4. In light of the promise of God's constancy in Psalm 139, describe the last time you experienced a "far side of the sea" season, when you felt God's unmistakable presence although you'd distanced yourself from Him.

5. Read Zephaniah 3:17. When do you think God sings loudest over you?

6. Take a few moments to rewrite Psalm 139, or just read it aloud, replacing all the personal pronouns with your own name. How does this exercise change your view of yourself?

4

THIS LOVE STORY MEANS HAVING TO SAY "I'M SORRY"

What Psalm 51 reveals about deep cleaning

our dirty hearts

A yes to life means an honest recognition
of our own evil, but it is also a yes to God,
who in the midst of our evil sustains us
and draws us into his righteousness.
—RICHARD FOSTER

Because I'm a big talker, my mouth tends to get me into trouble. Some of my verbal blunders are relatively benign, like the time I asked a total stranger who had a noticeably protruding tummy when her baby was due and she retorted, "I'm not pregnant!" (I learned the hard way not to ask a woman about her due date unless she's a close friend or is wearing one of those "Baby on Board" T-shirts!) But sometimes I wrap words around metaphorical daggers that have the potential to deeply wound others.

Recently the victim of one of my verbal knives called and asked me to go to lunch. Although much time had passed since I'd expressed my less-than-kind thoughts to a mutual acquaintance, anxiety welled up at the thought of seeing her again. I took a deep breath when I hung up the phone. Then the Holy Spirit added to my emotional distress by poking me and prompting, *It's time for you to admit what you did and tell her you're sorry.*

Justifications raced through my mind. *She's said some ugly things about me too, God! I'm not the only one who messed up here. Can't we just pretend it never happened, since she seems oblivious to my trash talk?* But God's Spirit was gently insistent, reminding me over and over again that I needed to own up to my dirty little secret of slander. By the time I walked into the restaurant where we had agreed to meet, my pulse was racing under the strain of lugging around the burden of remorse.

I suffered through small talk while nibbling on a salad, then when there was a lull in our conversation, I told her I needed to say something. The confession that followed was clumsy. My tongue got tangled up in the words. I felt my face get red. Tears sprang into the corners of my eyes, and my nose started to run. Mine wasn't one of those beautiful movie confessionals with violins playing in the background. It was messy. It was humiliating. It was awful. But it was also an enormous relief to take off that heavy backpack of guilt, to restore honest rapport with an old friend, and, most important, to be liberated from the shame wedged like a painful splinter in my relationship with God.

> Describe a time when you risked humiliation for the relief of being honest.

I like what C. S. Lewis says about confession: "A man who admits no guilt can accept no forgiveness."[1] In other words, we have to admit we're a mess to experience the perfect forgiveness and restoration God promises.

TURNING ON THE FAUCET OF FORGIVENESS

David was finally able to shrug off his own hefty backpack of guilt when, in Psalm 51, he owned up to his bad behavior. Acknowledging the truth about getting jiggy with Bathsheba must have triggered a sweet release from the pain of pretense. He no longer had to feign innocence or cover up the damning evidence. Surely David sighed with relief and wondered why he hadn't confessed the whole truth from the very beginning.

> Have mercy on me, O God,
>   according to your steadfast love;
> according to your abundant mercy
>   blot out my transgressions. *Psalm 51:1*

My friend Libby teaches a Sunday school class for five- and six-year-old boys in a small country church south of Nashville. Every time we get together, I can't wait to hear about the latest antics of her Presbyterian Huckleberry Finns! Her favorite student is a mischievous little imp named Bubba. Bubba has a strong Southern accent, lots of energy, and a fondness for wearing a miniature sheriff's uniform—complete with badge—to church.

One Sunday not long ago Bubba excused himself from class and went into the rest room. After several minutes passed, Libby thought he might need some help, so she knocked on the door and asked if he was okay. He replied that he was fine. But as Bubba's bathroom break stretched on and on, she started to worry. Just as she reluctantly decided to intrude on his privacy, the door swung open. Bubba swaggered out in his tiny vest, blue jeans, boots, and gun holster. Then with a John Wayne drawl, he said, "Sorry 'bout that, Miss Libby, but I was a little concentrated in there."

That hilariously direct and public confession stands in stark contrast to those times when we silently endure the private misery of spiritual "concentration," resulting from sin that clogs up the flow of God's grace in our lives. But much like Metamucil, a dose of confession rids our system of guilt and restores our comfort in God's presence. Can't you just hear the longing for relief that accompanies David's request?

> Wash me thoroughly from my iniquity,
>   and cleanse me from my sin!
>
> For I know my transgressions,
>   and my sin is ever before me. *Psalm 51:2–3*

I think verse 3 is especially poignant as David describes the inescapable reality of his choices. He observes Bathsheba, the beautiful woman he lured into adultery, eating breakfast across the table from him. He takes note of the empty spot marking where her husband, Uriah the Hittite, used to stand in military formation. He sees the guilt and condemnation written in the gaze of Joab, the king's right-hand man and an accessory to the crime.

Every time he opens his eyes, David is made painfully aware of the adultery and murder he committed, of the way he intentionally turned his back on God to fulfill his own selfish desires. David's sin wasn't a distant, blurry recollection that he could conveniently lock away into some mental closet; the evidence of his treachery was right in front of him, and he couldn't banish the image by himself.

THE BULL'S-EYE OF BAD BEHAVIOR

It's interesting that while David's adulterous dalliance with Bathsheba adversely impacted lots of lives, he still proclaims that God alone is the target of his transgressions:

> Against you, you only, have I sinned
> > and done what is evil in your sight,
> so that you may be justified in your words
> > and blameless in your judgment. *Psalm 51:4*

At these words I can imagine some of his royal attendants looking dismayed and thinking, *Well, I wouldn't exactly call adultery and murder private matters. You definitely owe poor, dead Uriah an apology too!* But the king's assessment is absolutely accurate. Because while some mistakes appear to be *internal,* with mostly personal consequences, and others appear to be *external,* with negative consequences for those around us, the heart of the matter is that *all* sin contradicts God Himself. When we choose our way over His way, we're essentially thumbing our nose in His holy face.

Furthermore, the apostle Paul adds that we don't belong to ourselves anymore anyway but have been bought by the inestimable price of Jesus's blood. Therefore we are called to glorify God instead of doing whatever we feel like doing.[2] So regardless of the details, God is always the bull's-eye of our rebellion. Opposing Him always peaks the Top Ten Bad Things About Sin list!

METHINKS YOU PROTEST TOO MUCH

Several years ago I spoke at a women's luncheon in downtown Nashville. I don't remember the title of the message, but I do remember the general idea was that we're a mess and we need God's mercy. I talked about how as flawed human beings we're prone to wander from our heavenly Father's will and affection and how, as a result, we desperately need God's grace to guide us back toward His plan and purpose for our lives.

After the luncheon I stood in the foyer of the church to chat with people on their way out. One woman—the wife of a well-known pastor—waited until we could speak privately, then remarked, "I think your topic was pertinent for most of the women here. However, I'm grateful to be fully sanctified, so I don't need God's grace to live a holy life anymore."

I grinned, certain she was teasing me. But when her steely facial expression didn't soften and I realized she was completely serious, my grin turned into a dumbfounded stare. I literally didn't know how to respond to someone who considered herself above God's reproach and no longer in need of His grace.

I can't imagine how miserable Mrs. I Don't Make Mistakes is behind closed doors. Her poor family; it must be hellish living with someone who won't say she's sorry, someone so bereft of humility that she's convinced she has attained perfection. I'll bet she doesn't even enjoy her own company because she surely hears whispers of self-recrimination while straining to keep that heavy halo in place. What a lonely life.

I think recognizing we're prone to err is foundational for healthy relationships with others and with God. Which brings us back to David's confession:

> Behold, I was brought forth in iniquity,
>   and in sin did my mother conceive me.
> Behold, you delight in truth in the inward being,
>   and you teach me wisdom in the secret heart.
> *Psalm 51:5–6*

Now David's not dissin' his mama here. This description of his innately flawed condition points to the doctrine of original sin—the reality that we don't become sinners; we're born sinners, thanks to the soul stain we inherited from Adam and Eve. The first sin took place in the Garden of Eden when Eve got seduced by a slithery liar and chowed down on the fruit from the one tree God had declared off-limits. With that one rebellious choice, she and Adam went from shameless nakedness to shame-filled hiding and blaming.[3] And humanity has been polluted ever since.

Quite frankly, when we don't recognize the reality of original sin—when we deny the truth of our own innate depravity—we minimize who God is.

THIS IS GOING TO TAKE A LOT OF SOAP

David's specific sanitation requests serve to further illustrate his recognition of the gravity of his offense:

Purge me with hyssop, and I shall be clean;

> wash me, and I shall be whiter than snow.

Let me hear joy and gladness;

> let the bones that you have broken rejoice.

Hide your face from my sins,

> and blot out all my iniquities. *Psalm 51:7–9*

"Hyssop" most likely referred to the herb we now call marjoram. This plant was used in an Old Testament cleansing ceremony for lepers or for Israelites who'd come in contact with a dead body.[4] Asking for hyssop was

---

PSALMS: THE INSIDE STORY

Seven of the psalms of lament are further classified as penitential psalms (6, 32, 38, 51, 102, 130, 143), and King David authored two of these (32, 51) after his affair with Bathsheba. Although Psalm 51 appears farther along in the Psalter, it was actually written first, after Nathan's confrontation helped David recognize his colossal blunder (see 2 Samuel 12:1–14). David wrote Psalm 32 later, after God had smoothed his sharp edges of grief and regret into gratitude and wisdom. Therefore, Psalm 32 has a much more contemplative theme and includes valuable life lessons that became clear to David in the season after his repentance in Psalm 51.

David's way of admitting his sin was supergross and thus needed an industrial-strength cleanser!

Which brings us back to the classification of this psalm; it's a psalm of lament, the expression of a heart crying out in grief. These lyrics don't communicate a superficial, Hallmark-card kind of "I'm sorry." This isn't an "Oops, God, sorry I goofed" confession. The language here indicates profound remorse. The words expose the misery of a man grappling with the horrific consequences of his own selfish behavior. They portray a contrite sinner weeping prostrate before a compassionate King.

And the submissive tone of Psalm 51 is what our apologies should sound like when we've thumbed our nose at almighty God. It's how I wish I had prayed long before I met my friend for lunch.

BE AFRAID, BE VERY AFRAID

After David soberly discusses his soul-laundering options with the Lord, he pleads with God not to leave him:

> Create in me a clean heart, O God,
>   and renew a right spirit within me.
> Cast me not away from your presence,
>   and take not your Holy Spirit from me.
> Restore to me the joy of your salvation,
>   and uphold me with a willing spirit.
> *Psalm 51:10–12*

The consequences of sin are scary. Sin wields the power to destroy families, ruin friendships, and divide churches. The shrapnel from its blast causes horrible collateral damage. When we choose to disobey God, we—and often the people we love most—will suffer terrible wounds. But sin's worst casualty is the way it implodes our intimacy with God, the way it disfigures us with the fear of abandonment.

When my friend Cindy used to discipline her son, he'd wail dramatically, "Don't leave me, Mama. Don't leave me!" The worst retribution Michael could imagine was his mother's absence. This dread lies at the core of David's cry too. *Purge me, spank me, renew me, fix me—do whatever You want, God. Just please don't leave me!*

Of course God promises never to leave His beloved; He will not abandon us in our anguish of repentance any more than Cindy would abandon Michael to his terror. David's unfounded fear of being cast away might have been rooted in his remembrance of how "the Spirit of the LORD departed from Saul" (1 Samuel 16:14), his ungodly royal predecessor (who was also a royal pain). Or it may have simply been David's way of saying "There's no way I can do life without You, God. If Your Holy Spirit doesn't help me, I'll inevitably make an even bigger mess the next time!"

OUR MESS CAN BE OUR MESSAGE

However, even amid the pain of confessing his major mistakes, David realizes that the miracle of God's redemption means good can rise out of the ashes of his sin. By honestly sharing the sin and forgiveness chapters of his story, he can motivate others to repent and run back to God's loving embrace:

> Then I will teach transgressors your ways,
> and sinners will return to you. *Psalm 51:13*

Bishop Lesslie Newbigin wrote, "The congregation is the hermeneutic of the Gospel."[5] In other words, day-to-day relationships are where and how the gospel is interpreted. We formulate our understanding of who God is largely through the lens of one another. When we as believers emulate David and admit our blunders, it not only opens the door to a restored relationship with God but also helps the watching world understand how amazing grace really is. Confession points to God as the true hero of our stories. Our forgiven trespasses become our testimony to His mercy. Our mess becomes our message.

MORNING WILL FOLLOW MIDNIGHT

My mom used to say, "It gets the darkest before the dawn." She cited that assurance—or something like it—when she drove me to piano practice, the bane of my childhood. I didn't like having to sit still inside for an hour, I didn't like the *ticktock* of the metronome, and I really didn't like the disappointment in my instructor's face after I mangled whatever arrangement she tried to teach me. However, when the bell chimed to end our session, I jumped off that shiny black bench with enthusiasm. Because

> ### PASS IT ON
> One research study on forgiveness found that "participants who believe they are forgiven by God were much more likely to forgive others unconditionally."[6] Apparently forgiveness is a contagious condition!

after each keyboard catastrophe, Mom took me to Faust's drugstore for a chocolate dipped ice-cream cone—the sugary sunrise to an emotional midnight!

I don't know if David itched to slip out of lyre lessons as a child, but he certainly understood the part about the brightest mornings coming after the darkest nights:

> Commute my death sentence, God, my salvation God,
>   and I'll sing anthems to your life-giving ways.
> Unbutton my lips, dear God;
>   I'll let loose with your praise.
> *Psalm 51:14–15, MSG*

Depending on which Old Testament professor you sit under or which commentary you read, at least one-third to one-half of the psalms are classified as songs of lament. And with the exception of Psalm 88, sooner or later they all evolve into praise choruses.[7] Which means when we sing the blues because of sin, God will eventually redeem our sad melodies into boogie-woogie choruses! Daybreak really will follow heartbreak.

Modern-day psalmist Michael Card explains the link between godly sorrow and celebration in compelling New Testament terms: "There is no worship without wilderness. There can be no worshipful joy of salvation until we have realized the lamentable wilderness of what we were saved from, until we begin to understand just what it cost Jesus to come and find us and be that perfect provision in the wilderness."[8]

The bottom line is, admitting our flaws leads to glorious intimacy with our heavenly Father.

GOD CELEBRATES SOFT HEARTS

I've had the privilege of hearing Max Lucado preach and teach many times through the years. One of his wise statements that lodged itself into my memory is, "If you've got to choose between a hard body and a soft heart, go for the soft heart every time!" As David winds down this wonderful song of repentance and praise, he too emphasizes the importance of having a tender heart:

> For you will not delight in sacrifice, or I would give it;
>> you will not be pleased with a burnt offering.
> The sacrifices of God are a broken spirit;
>> a broken and contrite heart, O God, you will not despise.
> *Psalm 51:16–17*

More than wanting to see us put wads of cash into the offering plate or volunteer to teach the Sunday school class nobody else wants (which constitute modern-day sacrifices and offerings), God desires us to come before Him with humility.

> ### PSALMS: THE INSIDE STORY
>
> The word *sacrifice* refers to a peace offering in the Old Testament sacrificial system and expressed communion with God; *burnt offerings* expressed dedication to God.[9]

Of course that doesn't mean we get off scot-free when it comes to tithing or volunteering at church. It simply means that the type of gifts we give God aren't as significant as the texture of our hearts. For instance, rather than reluctantly committing to be a small-group leader during a season when it doesn't work with your schedule, God would be more pleased if you honestly declined and then earnestly prayed for the small-group ministry. Rather than grumbling about giving extra money to the church mission fund, how about inviting your pastors and/or some missionaries over for dinner?

Our offerings to God aren't about earning His forgiveness or approval but about gratefully acknowledging His holy and perfect grace.

The tail end of Psalm 51 makes it clear that repentance isn't just for Lone Rangers but can impact an entire community. And I find it interesting that some scholars think these concluding verses were actually added long after David penned the first part. To be specific, they think the group petition that comes next was inserted as a sort of exclamation point after the Israelites returned to Jerusalem from captivity in Babylon to find the ramparts of their hometown ransacked. Thus, this explicit request to have the walls rebuilt:

> Do good to Zion in your good pleasure;
> build up the walls of Jerusalem;

then will you delight in right sacrifices,
> in burnt offerings and whole burnt offerings;
> then bulls will be offered on your altar. *Psalm 51:18–19*

Whether it's a poetical appendage or it originated with David, this portion is definitely a final plea for God's mercy and a promise to practice the art of confession. It makes the point that even when it comes to a gathering of believers, we must still admit our mistakes if we hope to enjoy God's favor.

A Prodigal's Promise

Years ago when a certain church voted to build a new sanctuary, the senior pastor insisted that the plans include kneelers in front of each pew. Because God's people are prone to fuss about things like the color of the carpeting and the size of the pulpit, quite a few grumbled about such an old-fashioned design. Legend has it they spouted things like "We're modern evangelicals; we shouldn't have anything that formal in the sanctuary!" and "Those stupid things always catch my heels and trip me when I'm trying to find a seat on Sunday!" and "What's next, smells and bells? If I want to kneel in church, I'll go to the cathedral downtown!"

Fortunately this senior pastor, a wonderful shepherd named Charles McGowan, was wise enough to stand firm against the naysayers. When the sanctuary of Christ Presbyterian Church in Nashville was finished, velvet-covered kneelers were permanent fixtures.

Many years later I joined the staff at CPC. And I can't tell you how many times on a Monday afternoon or a Thursday morning, when the sanctuary was dark and empty, I'd walk in, slide to my knees, and pray, "O Father, please forgive me for having such a rotten attitude. I need You to cleanse my heart and renew my mind and help me not to think cuss words about church members!" Or "Dear Lord, I'm sorry for worrying about what people think of me more than what You think of me. Please forgive me for bowing at the altar of human approval. Help me to walk in a way that honors You, no matter what anybody else thinks." Or "God, I'm such a goober! Remember what I asked You to forgive me for this morning? Well, I just did it again!"

I will always be grateful to my former pastor for sticking to his convictions, because I needed those kneelers. In fact, I'm pretty sure they had to replace the velvet on a few because I'd worn it thin! I'm convinced we could all benefit from bending to the posture of repentance.

Maybe you do your confessing while under the covers or while guiltily gobbling french fries in the privacy of your SUV. Or maybe it's been a while since you invited God in for a chat because you're embarrassed by the anger, resentment, sin, or failures cluttering up your heart. Instead of shoving it all into the bulging closet of "things to deal with later," why not just fling wide the door and let God make a clean sweep? I won't tell you it's easy to face your failures head-on, but I can promise you that, like David, you'll find new reasons to let loose with praise for God.

After I confessed my bad behavior to my old friend, I expected her to get upset and walk away. Or at least raise her eyebrows in polite disregard. Instead she smiled sincerely, then leaned over and hugged me. Although I'd cursed her, she blessed me. One of my favorite writers, Mark Twain, once said, "Forgiveness is the fragrance that the violet sheds on the heel that has crushed it." I found it to be a profoundly humbling yet beautiful experience to wear the fragrance of a flower I had trampled. And I've found the experience to be even sweeter when it's my Creator who's spraying the perfume of mercy.

God chooses to bless us even though we've all cursed Him with our disobedience. He is faithful to forgive and restore messy people who admit it.

⚊ The right-now relevance of Psalm 51 ⚊

God's love frees us from the muck and mire of guilt so we can walk in the sweet fragrance of the forgiven.

ENOUGH ABOUT ME. WHAT ABOUT YOU?

1. Psalm 51 records David's yearning to be reconciled with God after separating himself through sin. If you've ever experienced that kind of gaping distance between you and your heavenly Father, describe what you missed most about your relationship with Him.

2. Even though you may know with your head that God stands ready to forgive your sin, what do you really believe in your heart, and how is that reflected in your behavior?

3. "Love means never having to say you're sorry" is a famous line from the classic 1970 movie *Love Story,* starring Ali MacGraw and Ryan O'Neal. How would you respectfully counter this premise from a Christian perspective?

4. What are some of the reasons we hold back from confession—to God and others—even when we fully recognize the wrongness of our words or actions? What truths from Psalm 51 can help you move beyond that hesitation?

5. Read Psalm 51:16–17. Why do you think God prefers broken, contrite hearts over sacrifices? And what are some hallmarks of a broken, contrite heart?

6. Psalm 51 can be a helpful guide to cleaning out the crud between us and God. The basic steps are

    confession of specific sins,

    lamenting those sins,

    asking God's forgiveness, and

    praising God for His mercy.

Notice the acrostic CLAP, which might help you remember this guide to confession. When you have some time alone, consider using those principles to compose a personal paraphrase of Psalm 51.

5

WHEN GOD'S PEOPLE
LOSE THEIR GROOVE

What Psalm 42 teaches us about dealing

with our less-than-lovely emotions

God may be as much glorified by a weeping Jeremiah
as by an eagle-winged Ezekiel!
—CHARLES HADDON SPURGEON

This past fall I returned home from a week-long trip and fell into bed with a 104-degree fever and the kind of nausea that makes you certain you'll never eat so much as a Wheat Thin again. When I hauled myself out of bed to answer the ringing phone the next morning, I heard my mom's sweet voice explaining that Grandmom had died a few hours before. She was almost ninety-four, and her body and mind were weak, so we were mostly glad she'd gone to be with Jesus in glory. But she and my mother (her oldest daughter) were especially close, and it broke my heart to hear Mom so sad.

When I hung up the phone, it suddenly occurred to me that I hadn't looked in on my animals the night before. I was queasy and glassy-eyed with fever, and it was sleeting outside, but I didn't feel like I could wait any longer to check on my furry brood. (Someone looks in on them while I'm away, and they have automatic feed and water machines, but I still worry.) So I wriggled into a sweatshirt, slid my feet into clogs, and hobbled outside. My Jack Russell terriers, Harley and Dottie, were fine. I could also see that two of the Nigerian Dwarf goats were okay. You may be wondering about the goats. Well, my house sits on a little over an acre, which includes a steep hillside that's impossible to landscape. Some friends suggested getting goats to keep that area "mowed," and I agreed, thinking they'd also make cute, movable yard art. So I bought three wee girls: Scarlett, because I'm a fan of the movie *Gone with the Wind;* Ella, because I'm a fan of Ella Fitzgerald's music; and Sophie, because an acquaintance named her little girl Sophie, and I thought it had a nice ring to it. Of course, she doesn't know I named a goat after her child!

Anyway, Scarlett and Ella were bellowing on the hill all fat and sassy, but Sophie was nowhere to be seen. Then I peered into their stall and saw her lying on the ground. At first I thought, *Oh, little Sophie's taking a nap.* It took a few seconds for reality to penetrate the fog of my ache-addled brain, bringing the realization that her condition was a bit more permanent. Although I'm not nearly as attached to the goats as I am to the dogs, it was upsetting. Then it dawned on me I needed to move her away from the other animals in case she had a communicable disease. Frankly, I never had to deal with a goat cadaver before, and I wasn't sure where or how to transport her. Certain I was too weak to dig a hole—especially in the freezing rain—I reasoned, *I'll carry her up the hill and gently place her in the woods, then give her a proper burial with flowers and all in a few days when I'm stronger.*

I don't know if you've ever carried a stiff goat up a steep hill, but I found the task a bit more complicated than I expected. First of all, the slope was slick with ice, so I had a hard time keeping my balance. Second, I had to keep my arms perfectly straight because my awkward gait made Sophie swing, and if I bent my elbows, she bumped up against me, which, as you might imagine, was quite gross. Third, I had shuffled out of the house in my favorite "sick pants"—an old pair of sweatpants that no longer have any elastic in the waistband—and they were slipping down.

I'm not sure how to explain this tactfully, but here goes: I have always been a modest person, and therefore I almost always wear undergarments. I can only assume that the combination of grief and queasiness caused me to be forgetful about lingerie. Whatever the reason, I was sans underwear that particular morning, which made the drooping drawers more of a predicament. Furthermore, my house faces a busy highway, so I had little hope of escaping notice.

I faced a thorny dilemma: set Sophie on the ground and return to the house to change into different pants, or persist in the death march and allow my comfy ones to continue their downward slide. I deliberated, *If I set her down and one of her limbs falls off, I'm going to be really sick — maybe even padded-cell kind of sick. But if I keep going, my nether regions will be exposed.* Ultimately I chose sanity over modesty with the rationalization, *At least I'm far enough away from the road that it'll be more of a partial eclipse than a full moon.* If you happened to be one of the motorists scarred for life by my untimely revelation, I'm truly sorry. You have no idea how sorry.

After placing Sophie in a nice spot beneath a dogwood tree and yanking up the offending sweats, I walked back to the house with sagging shoulders and a heavy heart. I didn't feel like giving thanks; I felt like giving up. In one fell swoop I'd lost my grandmother, my goat, and my dignity. It was a really terrible, horrible, no good, very bad day!

I'm sure that, like me, you have experienced days…or weeks…or years when it seemed like everything was going wrong, and your soul was drooping as a result.

> What happened on your most recent terrible, horrible, no good, very bad day?

Maybe you've slogged through difficulties like a catastrophic illness, the death of a loved one, a divorce, or bills that added up to more than the balance in your bank account. No matter how the details of your story differ from mine, I'm certain you can easily recall a season when you were overwhelmed with disappointment and sadness. When it seemed your prayers for relief weren't getting past the ceiling. When you lost your spiritual groove while hiking up steep emotional hills. Thankfully, the gospel frees us from pretending everything in our life is hunky-dory when it's not. God doesn't demand that we be perpetually perky.

THE SOUND OF MISERY

On those days when I'd rather crawl back into the nest of my bed than wing my way into a dangerous and disappointing world, I'm especially grateful that God's Word includes stories about people who could empathize with my misery. Scripture reveals that even those whom God anointed for leadership went through serious slumps. After an immature Moses lost his temper and killed a bad guy, he retreated to the boonies to hide out and wrangle sheep.[1] A little while later in the Old Testament, when a mean chick named Jezebel threatened the prophet Elijah, he responded by hightailing it out of town, hiding under a broom tree, and asking God to take his life. Worse still, his terrible, horrible, no good, very bad day took place immediately *after* his best day, when he got to watch God pour out His glory on Mount Carmel.[2] You'd think Elijah wouldn't act like such a wimp when he'd just been privy to God's supernatural power!

But God wasn't absent in these situations, despite the lack of admirable behavior displayed by Moses and Elijah. Instead of ditching Moses in the desert, God sent a flaming topiary to remind him of his calling and renew his spiritual vigor.[3] Rather than abandon Elijah to his pity party, God impressed him to take a nap and sent angels to restore his energy with tasty snacks. Then God appeared to him in a soft voice. And the whisper of I AM was enough to rouse Elijah from his depression.[4]

The encouraging promise of God's company in cruddy seasons is also apparent in one of the most melancholy tunes in the Psalter, Psalm 42:

> As a deer thirsts for streams of water,
>   so I thirst for you, God.
> I thirst for the living God.
>   When can I go to meet with him?
> Day and night, my tears have been my food.

People are always saying,
  "Where is your God?" *Psalm 42:1–3, NCV*

Notice that the psalmist compares himself to a deer and not a camel. In other words, he doesn't have a hump filled with fluid to satisfy his own thirst. He's not self-sufficient; he's vulnerable. His parched anxiety is evidenced by the cry *"When?"* And his plight is exacerbated by ridicule from the local peanut gallery in verse 3. Because God's ways are often inscrutable to mankind, believers are susceptible to scorn when they choose faith in the ugly face of reality.

I have to be honest here: trusting that God will appear with a canteen while you're trudging through the desert with your tongue hanging out does seem a tad optimistic. Although we can trust God to be absolutely faithful, based on His Word and biblical history, it's still pretty normal to question *when* He'll show up if we're gasping in the wasteland!

NO NEED TO HIDE A BROKEN HEART

Thankfully, we don't have to mask our desperate thirst for relief, as this songwriter demonstrates by honestly unloading even more stuff off his chest:

When I remember these things,
  I speak with a broken heart.
I used to walk with the crowd
  and lead them to God's Temple
  with songs of praise. *Psalm 42:4, NCV*

Psalm 42 was penned by the sons of Korah. These guys originated from the tribe of Levi and were given the task of leading worship through music, first in the tent of meeting, which was where the Israelites worshiped before they had a brick-and-mortar building, and then in the temple when it was constructed.[5] Verse 4 is an obvious lament for those days, a nostalgic longing for happier times when they led an ancient choir of God's people.

My guess is, you can relate. While we each have trudged through some type of desert on occasion, we've also experienced glorious vacations from difficulty. Times when we cheerfully told other people about God's goodness to us. Times when we couldn't wait to discuss Bible study homework with our girlfriends at church. Times when a praise chorus sprang from our lips the minute our feet hit the floor each morning.

But then heartache hit, and we felt like frauds as we continued to mouth words of praise while our souls writhed in anguish. It's hard not to wonder why God allows suffering, especially when you're dutifully singing the chorus of "How Great Is Our God" on Sunday morning while simultaneously evading the kind gaze of friends in an effort not to cry.

PSALMS: THE INSIDE STORY

Because so many of the psalms are classified as laments, these Old Testament songs probably sounded like a blues record in their original format, making David kind of like the precursor to B. B. King!

Most scholars believe two of the especially bluesy tunes, Psalms 42 and 43, were originally two halves of one poem, because early manuscripts link them together and Psalm 43 wasn't given an individual title.[6]

I'm so thankful this lament (and many others like it) is included in the psalms. Because instead of disowning disillusioned people, God presents in Psalm 42 an engraved invitation for us to express our sorrow. Our Redeemer permits us to bring *everything*—disappointment, frustration, and even whining—to Him as an act of worship. And from those emotional ashes, God creates an exquisite and acceptable offering unto Himself. There is no shame in confessing we feel far away from God; it certainly doesn't surprise Him! I believe the first step to getting our groove back is being honest enough to admit we've lost it.

A Brief Detour Back to Hope

After looking back with longing to "the way we were," it's as if the song-writer pinches himself back to reality and exclaims, "Oh yeah! Now I remember that God said He would never leave me or forsake me!" He stops fretting when he refocuses on God's goodness.

> Why am I so sad?
> > Why am I so upset?
> I should put my hope in God
> > and keep praising him,
> > my Savior and my God. *Psalm 42:5–6, NCV*

But all too quickly he turns his face from God and back toward his problems:

> I am very sad.
> > So I remember you where the Jordan River begins,
> near the peaks of Hermon and Mount Mizar.
> Troubles have come again and again, sounding like waterfalls.
> > Your waves are crashing all around me. *Psalm 42:6–7, NCV*

By bringing to mind the Jordan River racing downhill toward the Sea of Galilee, the psalmist communicates a sense of being emotionally pummeled. In its descent down the slopes of Mount Hermon—the dominant peak in a mountain range perhaps known as Mizar in ancient times—the Jordan is a mighty current, crashing over boulders in its haste to get to the valley below. It's not a gentle stream where you would rest your tired feet after a long hike; it's more like a mini–Niagara Falls!

I grew up in central Florida, where we went to the beach every chance we got. And one of my favorite activities was body-surfing—leaping into a cresting wave just before it broke, then riding the powerful white water to shore with my hands in front of me like Superman. Now that I live in Tennessee, I don't get to the beach nearly as often. But when I do, I still love body-surfing. Only now that I'm older and less agile, I tend to miss as many waves as I catch. Which means sometimes I end up underneath the wave. Instead of a grin-inducing, graceful kind of flying experience, it's more of a tumbling-head-over-heels, completely-disoriented, lungs-bursting, eventually-being-flattened-on-the-gritty-bottom kind of experience. When I finally stagger to my feet and start emptying the sand from my bathing suit, I'm quite sure I resemble a cat emerging from a washing machine. Being hammered by H_2O puts me in mind of the picture painted by verses 6 and 7.

However, there's a silver lining in the whiny cloud above. When the psalmist describes the surge washing over him as "your waves," he's alluding to God's absolute sovereignty. Which reminds me of David's assertion in Psalm 119:75: "I know, O LORD, that your rules are righteous, and that in faithfulness you have afflicted me." Both David and the Korah clan understood that God's providence can include pain, that difficulties can be a divinely plowed path inviting us to experience Him more fully.

A LIGHT IN THE DUNGEONS OF DESPAIR

The next section of Psalm 42 is bittersweet—bitter because of the continued frustration and pain being expressed, yet sweet because of the way it reveals a believer honestly grieving in his conversation with God. These three verses rip the mask off artificial prayers filled with fake happiness and pithy sentiments. They remind us of the freedom we have to pour out the messy sorrows of our hearts to our heavenly Father instead of trying to suppress the sad stuff.

> The LORD shows his true love every day.
>> At night I have a song,
>> and I pray to my living God.
> I say to God, my Rock,
>> "Why have you forgotten me?
> Why am I sad
>> and troubled by my enemies?"
> My enemies' insults make me feel
>> as if my bones were broken.
> They are always saying,
>> "Where is your God?" *Psalm 42:8–10, NCV*

Do you ever wonder why, since our Savior consented to suffering, we try to avoid it at all costs? "For it was fitting that he, for whom and by whom all things exist, in bringing many sons to glory, should make the founder of their salvation perfect through suffering" (Hebrews 2:10).

Most of us do everything we can to sidestep the slightest twinge of discomfort. But dodging pain makes for an anxious existence. And trying to cruise through life in the single gear of "happy" makes for an ineffective witness. How can we expect others to connect with our faith story when we've edited out the hard parts, the parts they most identify with?

Unfortunately, our society tends to respond to legitimate human sorrow with either discomfort or disdain. Brokenhearted people are expected to keep their grief tucked in lest it provoke others to get in touch with theirs. Or else they're told to find a quarter and call someone who cares. Even the Christian culture has the propensity to censor pain. I grew up surrounded by believers who sincerely thought sadness was a bad emotion, that God's people shouldn't admit we suffer because doing so might jeopardize His reputation as a redeemer. So my journey into the language of lament has been a slow learning process. I've found the best tutors, apart from Scripture, to be the stumbling saints who've gone before me.

As a college coed, I was encouraged to be more candid about my own struggles after reading how C. S. Lewis (surely one of the most gifted Christian writers in history) struggled with debilitating sadness and questioned God after losing his wife, Joy, to cancer. A few years later I was schooled in the subjects of empathy and concern while studying how the prolific pastor Charles Haddon Spurgeon battled severe depression. Despite the fact that at the height of his ministry twenty-five thousand people bought copies of his sermons every week and that he got to preach to ten million people before his death in 1892, Spurgeon still had days when he didn't want to get out of bed. Following one of his darkest moments, he said, "There are dungeons beneath the castles of despair."[8]

DON'T HOLD IT ALL IN

Researchers are learning that a good cry can actually help us feel better, because "tears appear to reduce tensions, remove toxins, and increase the body's ability to heal itself."[7] Consider it yet another way God cares for us even in our grief.

The testimonies of sincere strugglers like these helped reshape my distortion of sad. But my education is certainly not finished. My dad's recent bout with cancer and my stepdad's decline into the mental prison of Alzheimer's have provided new opportunities to express honest grief in prayer. I'm learning to trust that God's throne room is a safe place to store all my tear-stained stuff.

Hanging On to Hope

Psalm 42 concludes by repeating the restorative questions of verse 5 (also repeated in Psalm 43:5), which are all about hanging on to hope even when life is unbearably hard:

> Why am I so sad?
>> Why am I so upset?
> I should put my hope in God
>> and keep praising him,
>> my Savior and my God. *Psalm 42:11, NCV*

Some of the most joyful people I know—certainly the most believable believers—are those who've waded honestly through woundedness. Those who've trudged through difficult seasons only to come out communing with God more deeply.

Several years ago I was teaching at a retreat where a radiant woman sat on the front row. I was so intrigued by the noticeable joy in her countenance—she was practically luminescent—that I asked her to meet me for coffee after the program. After a few minutes of small talk, I told her I'd never met anyone who glowed quite like her. She thanked me for the compliment and then told me her story.

She had married young and married badly. Her husband was abusive, and after suffering for years she finally found the courage to leave him, determined to protect their three young sons from his violent behavior. But while they were separated and the divorce was pending, he still had visitation rights. One weekend he defiantly announced that he was taking the kids camping. She felt uneasy about the trip, yet she had no choice but to let them go. Her estranged husband then took two of those precious little boys into the woods and killed them before turning the gun on himself.

With tears rolling down her face, she went on to celebrate God's grace in the midst of unbelievable sadness. She shared details of His compassion, how her sons hadn't suffered and how the baby had been spared because she had insisted he was too little to sleep outside. She described how she had met and fallen in love with her second husband—a godly, kind man—and how they had recently had her fourth child. With sparkling eyes she explained how tragedy had taught her to put her hope in eternal things and to consider every moment with her friends and family a gift from God's hand. And deep within my spirit I knew she wasn't simply reciting platitudes; she meant every word.

Authentic joy is often forged in the kiln of ache. Horrible messes really can lead to hope-filled messages.

OUR EVER-PRESENT HELP IN TROUBLE

On the afternoon of that terrible, horrible, no good, very bad day when both my grandmother and my goat died—and my nether regions made an embarrassing, unscheduled appearance—God hugged me. I was in a heap on the couch, bawling my eyes out, when I sensed His arms around me. Of course I couldn't see God, but His presence was as tangible as the heat coming from the fireplace. And the really cool thing was, I didn't feel any shame. I didn't feel the need to pretend like everything was okay or to rein in my sorrow. I just sobbed, and He held me until my shoulders stopped shaking.

I am convinced that trusting God with our pain and disappointment leads to greater intimacy with Him. When we tell God where and why it hurts, we will experience divine embraces that last until our souls stop quivering. We will hear comforting whispers that mute our cries of distress. We will sense nail-scarred hands reaching down to tilt our faces toward Him, followed by the promise, "I'm right here… I'll never leave you."

When we let it all out and tell God exactly how we feel, we will come to truly believe that rather than watching at a distance until we pull ourselves together, our Redeemer draws close to brokenhearted people.

The right-now relevance of Psalm 42

God's love frees us to grieve honestly while never losing sight of the supernatural hope we have in Him.

ENOUGH ABOUT ME. WHAT ABOUT YOU?

1. Read Psalm 56:8. In light of God's promise to store our tears in a bottle, has He needed a small, medium, or large container for you this past year? What has He recorded in His book about your sorrows?

2. The Bible records ancient leaders like Job, David, and Jeremiah weeping and even describes Jesus crying over the spiritual blindness of Jerusalem.[9] So why do you think so many Christians seem uncomfortable with tears?

3. Read 2 Corinthians 12:7–10. How would you sum up Paul's point in your own words?

4. Read Hebrews 2:18 and 2 Corinthians 1:3–4. Describe a situation where God used a sad chapter of your story to encourage someone walking through a difficult season, or tell about a time when someone drew on his or her own sorrowful experience to offer you real comfort.

5. Read Psalms 42 and 43 together. What descriptive titles would you give to the beginning, middle, and end of these sixteen verses?

6. Read Revelation 21:1–4. How would you explain this passage to a kindergarten Sunday school class? What relevance does it have in your life today?

6

FAITHFUL FURY

How Psalm 83 shows what God can do

with a little well-placed anger

Silence encourages the tormentor,
never the tormented.
—ELIE WIESEL

M ost of my adult life has been spent surrounded by other believers. All but one of my jobs since college has involved working directly with churches and ministries. The majority of my friends love Jesus. Many of the conversations I have in coffee shops are about the Bible. And while I truly appreciate the camaraderie I have with other Christians, several years ago I began to feel like something was lacking. I missed interacting with people outside the family of faith. I began to feel like a cloistered Christian.

So I joined a mountain-bike racing team to meet people who didn't yet believe God loved them. My new bike-riding friends were very different than my work friends. When they hit a root while careening down a hillside and were thrown over the handlebars, they used much more colorful expressions than *darn* or *shoot*. Prerace meals didn't begin with a prayer. Our competitions weren't polite affairs like the backyard barbecues I enjoyed with co-workers. And despite arduous training rides, numerous cuts and bruises, and exorbitant expenses (you can buy a nice car for the same purchase price as some high-tech bikes), I never won a race.

But I did manage a top-three finish at the Iron Horse Bicycle Classic in Durango, Colorado—one of the oldest and most prestigious races on the circuit. I was so nervous before it began that I seriously considered sneaking under the ropes and backing out! Since I was squashed in the middle of the group, I had no choice except to pedal madly like everyone else when the starter's gun went off. Those mass starts are like wedging ten people in a phone booth, then telling them the last one standing will get a million dollars; it's a rough and sweaty free-for-all!

However, within a hundred yards the trail curved ominously uphill, and the crowd thinned, along with the oxygen. Pretty soon all you could hear were bike gears grinding under the strain of ascent and riders gasping for breath. Evidently, being intimidated had given me a surge of adrenaline, because I soon found myself miraculously near the front of the pack, about fifteenth or sixteenth in a field of two hundred. And I probably would've been content to stay in that position had a cheater not elbowed past me and, in her obsessive quest for victory, knocked another girl down with a big shove and a bad word.

After making sure the rider sprawled in the dirt was okay, I took off after that cussing stinker. Something about her bad sportsmanship ignited the competitive fire in me! With head down, legs pumping furiously, and a white-knuckle grip on the handlebars, I pursued her relentlessly. I didn't have a plan for what to do if I caught up to her; I was just mad. I climbed past other riders as if they were standing still. I flew down rocky descents without touching the brakes. I like to think Lance Armstrong would have been impressed with my bike-racing prowess that day!

When was the last time you got really mad because of someone else's meanspirited behavior?

Eventually I caught up with the jerk in the green jersey. With an angry sideways glance, I pedaled around her. She tried to regain her position when the trail widened, so I increased the pace in order to maintain the lead. It took every single bit of skill and energy I had to stay in front of her. My heart rate was so high I'm surprised I didn't vibrate right out of the saddle. But at the end of the contest, I rolled triumphantly through the finish line a few feet ahead of the bully, clinching third place!

I'm not sure if vengeance is justified in mountain-bike racing, but there are definitely times when it's appropriate for Christians to get ticked off. Just as God doesn't require Christians to be perpetually happy, He also doesn't require us to pretend like we never get heated. Our Redeemer allows our feelings of "sad" *and* "mad" to be expressed. In fact, the Bible records numerous rants and raves, from Moses confronting Pharaoh in "hot anger" to Nehemiah getting peeved about how the wealthy Israelites were exploiting the poor.[1]

TIME TO MAKE SOME NOISE

Some of the more emotive "mad" language of Scripture can be found in the imprecatory passages of the psalms (to imprecate is to call down curses on someone else[2]). And one of the most withering imprecations can be found in Psalm 83, which was penned by Asaph, King David's worship director.[3] But before Asaph started firing verbal missiles, he sang a complaint:

> O God, do not keep silence;
>> do not hold your peace or be still, O God!
> For behold, your enemies make an uproar;
>> those who hate you have raised their heads.
> They lay crafty plans against your people;
>> they consult together against your treasured ones.
> They say, "Come, let us wipe them out as a nation;
>> let the name of Israel be remembered no more!"
> For they conspire with one accord;
>> against you they make a covenant—

the tents of Edom and the Ishmaelites,

Moab and the Hagrites,

Gebal and Ammon and Amalek,

Philistia with the inhabitants of Tyre;

Asshur also has joined them;

they are the strong arm of the children of Lot.

Psalm 83:1–8

Israel was often surrounded by murderous pagans intent on its destruction, as God's ancient people had an unusually long list of enemies: the Hittites, the Amorites, the Canaanites, the Moabites, the Perizzites, the Hivites, and the Jebusites. That's in addition to the Gazites, the Ekronites, the Avvites, the Gebalites, the Geshurites, and a whole lot of other *ites*![4] Furthermore, the bad guys had a habit of banding together when they picked on the Israelites, so it was rarely a fair fight.

All that bullying is the catalyst behind Asaph's cry for help here. He's carved out a huge SOS in the desert sand and is looking toward heaven, crying, "Jehovah, You've gotta help us, or we're gonna get beat like a drum!"

Then Asaph remembers he's on God's team, which ensures final victory. He thinks, *Those bullies are going to get what's coming to them one day!* A sly grin plays at the corners of his mouth and a gleam twinkles in his eyes as he begins to envision his persecutors' comeuppance:

Do to them as you did to Midian,

as to Sisera and Jabin at the river Kishon,

who were destroyed at En-dor,

who became dung for the ground.

Make their nobles like Oreb and Zeeb,

all their princes like Zebah and Zalmunna,

who said, "Let us take possession for ourselves
of the pastures of God." *Psalm 83:9–12*

It's hard not to smile at the reference to Midian because that story is bound to be on every underdog's favorite-battle list! It's when an Israelite leader named Gideon put his trust in God's power and unpredictably conquered a massive enemy stronghold with a motley crew of three hundred soldiers carrying water jugs and flashlights.[5] It's also amusing that

---

PSALMS: THE INSIDE STORY

Although Psalm 83 includes the calling down of curses, it is classified as a psalm of complaint or lament rather than as an imprecatory psalm. A total of eighteen psalms include an element of imprecation, but only six of those—Psalms 55, 59, 69, 79, 109, and 137—are generally classified as imprecatory.[6] It should also be noted that most of the imprecations voiced in the psalms can also be found elsewhere in Scripture, describing the fate of those who consistently oppose God.

Asaph brings up Jabin and his army commander, Sisera. Their defeat came at the hands of the only female judge in Israel's history, a great leader named Deborah, and a tent-peg-wielding woman named Jael.[7] It's as if the psalmist sticks his tongue out at his enemies from the safety of God's shadow and taunts, "Nanny, nanny, boo, boo. You got crushed by two *chicks*!"

WEARING JEHOVAH'S TEAM JERSEY

I imagine Asaph's smile fading and the furrow in his brow deepening as his indignation increases:

O my God, make them like whirling dust,
    like chaff before the wind.
As fire consumes the forest,
    as the flame sets the mountains ablaze,
so may you pursue them with your tempest
    and terrify them with your hurricane! *Psalm 83:13–15*

Asaph uses dramatic imagery to urge God to destroy His enemies. He chants for them to be thrown into a washing machine and put on the spin cycle, for them to be toasted like marshmallows over an open flame, and for them to be trampled by a tornado!

The language here reminds me of how sports fanatics rage against an opposing team. A few of my girlfriends from church are rabid Nashville Predators hockey fans. One of their husbands introduced them to the sport, but they've long since surpassed the men in their lives with their devotion to Tennessee's NHL franchise. They're season-ticket holders, wear Preds paraphernalia, and even study the stats of opposing teams. They were horrified when they found out I'd never been to a single game and insisted that I join them as soon as I could. So one night a few months ago I did.

But first they made me slip a sweltering, nylon, blue and gold jersey over my cute outfit. Then they drilled me in hockey facts on the way to the arena. I was bemused by their zeal and didn't understand what all the commotion was about…until I started watching the game. Within ten minutes I was cheering and waving a sign. By the third period I was on my feet, screaming for one of our guys to smash the opposing team's skater into the boards!

So I can't help but picture Asaph, our fiery worship leader, wearing a Jehovah's Team jersey, waving a foam finger, and screaming for his Creator to crush the bad guys!

However, before we get going too fast down this cranky path, it would behoove us to review God's boundaries about getting irritated. The bad news for hotheads is that there are more verses warning against anger than advocating it. For instance, the apostle Paul advises us to let our heavenly Father fight our battles: "My friends, do not try to punish others when they wrong you, but wait for God to punish them with his anger. It is written: 'I will punish those who do wrong; I will repay them,' says the Lord" (Romans 12:19, NCV). Paul also says elsewhere to Christians that "you must put them all away: anger, wrath, malice, slander, and obscene talk from your mouth" (Colossians 3:8).

And his buddy James states we're supposed to be poky when it comes to getting peeved: "Know this, my beloved brothers: let every person be quick to hear, slow to speak, slow to anger; for the anger of man does not produce the righteousness of God" (1:19–20).

So how come Asaph was allowed to say such acerbic things about his enemies? Why was it all right for the psalmists and not for us? My favorite commentator on the psalms, Tremper Longman, explains this conundrum with a lesson on the progressive revelation of Scripture. He says that whereas God clearly called His people to be holy and separate in the Old Testament—and sometimes even ordered the Israelites to fight with their enemies—the New Testament now charges Christians to love our enemies (see Matthew 5:43–44; Luke 6:27–36) and fight against "spiritual forces of evil in the heavenly realms" (Ephesians 6:12, NIV).[8] Modern spiritual missiles are supposed to be aimed at Satan and his schemes, not particular people groups. Calling down curses on individuals just doesn't reflect the radical grace Jesus poured out on us in the New Covenant!

ANGER AND AFFECTION AREN'T MUTUALLY EXCLUSIVE

Although Asaph didn't have any firsthand experience with the New Covenant, he was a recipient of Jehovah's mercy. Which is why he was able

to show concern regarding the spiritual condition of his foes in the last
stanza:

> Knock the breath right out of them, so they're gasping
> for breath, gasping, "GOD."
> Bring them to the end of their rope,
> and leave them there dangling, helpless.
> Then they'll learn your name: "GOD,"
> the one and only High God on earth.
>
> *Psalm 83:15–18,* MSG

I used to get so frustrated by my little brother's rebellion when I was
in high school and college. I frequently encouraged my mom to be stricter
with him because I thought he needed harsher consequences. But oh how
I hated it when he got spanked. All the annoyance that had collected in
my big-sister heart dissipated at the sight of John Price's tear-streaked face.
I have to wonder if Asaph felt that same kind of sympathy in light of the
way he concludes Psalm 83: "Then they'll learn your name: 'GOD,' the
one and only High God on earth." It's as if all his resentment has been
distilled into one desire—for his tormentors to know who God is.

Have you ever tallied up people who don't share your positions on
moral issues like abortion and homosexuality in a mental "enemy" col-
umn? Do you expend as much energy hoping they'll come to know the
Lord as you do hoping they'll be proved wrong? Have you ever felt anything close to love for your enemies?

One of the most familiar stories in the Gospels about righteous anger
underscores Jesus's deep affection for mankind:

When it was almost time for the Jewish Passover Feast, Jesus went
to Jerusalem. In the Temple he found people selling cattle, sheep,

and doves. He saw others sitting at tables, exchanging different kinds of money. Jesus made a whip out of cords and forced all of them, both the sheep and cattle, to leave the Temple. He turned over the tables and scattered the money of those who were exchanging it. Then he said to those who were selling pigeons, "Take these things out of here! Don't make my Father's house a place for buying and selling!" *John 2:13–16, NCV*

Jesus wasn't just seething about the commercialism polluting the temple; He was livid that money-changers were charging exorbitant fees and making it impossible for poor people to worship (see also Matthew 21:12–13; Luke 19:45–46). His image-bearers were being exploited. Our Savior directed His anger at the barrier separating people from God's love.

We should do the same.

Christians should be incensed about such horrors as pornography, genocide disguised as ethnic cleansing, and the child sex trade. We should get angry when other people are abused and exploited. And we should do something about it.

In the preface of *Night*, his powerful book about the Holocaust, Elie Wiesel explains why he had to write about the horrifying experience of being tortured and losing his loved ones in Nazi death camps: "I only know that without this testimony, my life as a writer—or my life, period—would not have become what it is: that of a witness who believes he has a moral obligation to try to prevent the enemy from employing one last victory by allowing his crimes to be erased from human memory."[9]

> **ANGER ISSUES**
> A Chinese proverb cautions, "Have no unreasonable anger, but be not without righteous anger."

Wiesel got mad about the millions of Jews murdered during one of the darkest chapters of human history. Then he did something about it. We too can take redemptive actions after we take offense. Christians can get involved with organizations working to free children who've been sold into slavery and volunteer at shelters for battered women. We can lead the charge against oppression and cruelty. Our active indignation could even inspire the watching world to be more intentional about eradicating evil.

And ultimately, if our outrage leads to change that helps restore people into a loving, healing relationship with Jesus, it can be described as righteous.

FOES WHO COULD BE FRIENDS

I'm so glad God gives us the freedom to fuss. It does my imperfect heart good to read about psalmists getting their britches in a bunch! I'm also thankful our Abba has given us the green light to get riled up and combat wickedness and heresy. Alas, I must admit I usually get more offended when someone slanders me than when someone slanders God.

Not too long ago a book critic gave one of my manuscripts a scathing review. She described the content as "fluff" and stereotyped me as a literary lightweight. While her comments stung, I respected her right to voice a negative opinion; that's part of being published. What I didn't appreciate was her choice to print inaccuracies that made it obvious she hadn't read one complete chapter, much less the whole book. The way she fabricated things that weren't in the text really bothered me. Soon after reading her insults, I gave birth to a small grudge. Before long that grudge grew into a monster.

I fantasized about exposing her book-review fraud. I pondered what she'd feel like if someone filleted one of her romance novels. I thought about telling her off—with appropriate Christian semantics and a calm voice, of course. I empathized with the psalmists' imprecatory wishes about the annihilation of their adversaries. I dreamed about this woman wearing a full-body rash. Then someone e-mailed me a picture of her. And she looked like a normal housewife…like somebody's mom…like half the women I go to church with. I was ashamed at how quickly my resentment toward someone who wasn't evil at all had bloomed. Toward someone who was probably a lot like me—a messy girl who loves Jesus and makes mistakes.

The Holy Spirit whispered a gentle rebuke as I stared at the computer screen. He reminded me that while God permits us to express anger, we aren't supposed to sin in the process: "When you are angry, do not sin, and be sure to stop being angry before the end of the day" (Ephesians 4:26, NCV).

I don't know if you've been humiliated, betrayed, or lied about lately. But I do know it's a good idea to hit your knees before punching a wall. It's a good idea to ask yourself, "Is my motive to be *right* or to be *righteous*?" before lambasting whoever's hurt you. And remembering that your rival has a bumpy and bruised heart much like the one beating in your own chest might help temper your temper.

The right-now relevance of Psalm 83

God's love frees us to express righteous indignation and anger, then channel that emotion into redemptive action.

ENOUGH ABOUT ME. WHAT ABOUT YOU?

1. Describe the last time you were red-in-the-face furious. Now describe a situation where you think you displayed righteous

anger. What are the similarities and dissimilarities between the two mad moments?

2. How would you describe the tension between being legitimately outraged and resting in God's omniscience?

3. Read Psalm 69:16–28. Have you ever experienced feelings similar to these? If so, how did God specifically comfort you and assuage your anger?

4. Describe a recent situation where you lost your temper with someone only to realize later that you weren't really mad at him or her but were mad about something else altogether. Perhaps you scowled at the grocery clerk who was taking so long to scan your items only to realize later you weren't actually frustrated with her but with your husband who just phoned to say he was going to be late to dinner again. Then list a few ways you can be more intentional about being mad at the sin undermining

human relationships than with individuals who sometimes disappoint and hurt you.

5. Read Proverbs 12:16. How would you restate this verse in your own words?

6. Do you think the imprecatory psalms should be used in modern worship? If so, how do you see them being incorporated? Should they be sung, prayed in public, or used in some other manner?

7

WE'RE IN GREAT HANDS

How Psalm 110 points to a future free of fear

For the disciple, God is no other
than as he is seen in the person of Jesus:
"He who sees me sees the Father" (John 14:9).
—BRENNAN MANNING

In recent weeks my nearest neighbor has started knocking on my back door and bedroom windows at night. Since I live alone in a cottage out in the country, you might be thinking, *How nice that she has such a friendly neighbor!* But this poor fellow was literally kicked in the head by a mule when he was younger, which left him a few fries short of a Happy Meal. Plus, he's been arrested numerous times over the years for illegal drug use and burglary, and he only recently got out of prison for committing a violent crime against another female in our tiny community. As you might imagine, his nocturnal visits leave me feeling rather tense.

Fortunately, local law enforcement is sympathetic to my situation, and the newly elected sheriff even took the time to pay a personal visit. He walked through my house and backyard, taking note of areas where I would be most vulnerable and advising me on how to better protect myself. Then he assured me his deputies were monitoring the situation closely and encouraged me to call 911 immediately the next time "Sling Blade" came calling.

Several nights after Sheriff Long's visit, I arrived home after dark. The entire time I walked from the garage to the house, I had an ominous feeling. Like a kid walking through a cemetery on a dare, I squared my shoulders and whistled while striding down the stone steps and across the courtyard to my back door. Resisting the urge to look over my shoulder, I jiggled the key that now didn't seem to fit the lock. The deadbolt finally pulled back, and the door squeaked in protest as I pushed it open. I breathed a sigh of relief, thankful to be inside.

My relief was short-lived. Moments later as I was talking on the cell phone with my aunt Darlene, the back doorbell rang. I shrieked, "Oh no, it's him!" because in the four years I've lived in this quaint cottage, my nutty neighbor is the only person who's come to the back door at night without calling first.

Darlene shrieked back, "What do you want me to do?"

"Nothing," I replied. (Since she lives in Florida, I didn't think she'd be of much assistance.) "I need to call 911!" But I couldn't get the iPhone to cooperate because my fingers were trembling too much to work the touchscreen. I tossed it on the bed, frantically grabbed another phone, and punched 911 as fast as I could. I waited impatiently for a response, only to realize precious seconds later that I hadn't pressed Send, so the call hadn't gone through!

By the time an operator answered with the words, "What is the nature of your emergency?" I was quivering like a naked person in a blizzard. I blurted my name, address, and emergency. Then the operator (whose sleepy tone suggested he was on Benadryl) began to ask additional, seemingly trivial questions. I tried to answer his queries like a dutiful citizen—this was the first time I'd called 911, so I wanted to do a good job—but after a few minutes of obedience, I felt compelled to interrupt the survey and beg, "Please send the police. I think they're parked right down the road!" He unhurriedly explained they were on their way. I thought, *If you'd just told me that earlier, I would have been less panicky and more polite.*

Moments later he informed me that officers were at my front door. I ran through the house and flung open the door to find three deputies waiting. Two squad cars were parked diagonally across the highway to block traffic, their flashing blue lights illuminating the porch like a cerulean disco. I exclaimed, "I'm so glad you're here!" and plopped down on the steps, my knees suddenly too weak to hold me up. I don't think I've ever being happier to have guests. Those men in blue (well, their uniforms are actually green and yellow) were one of the most appreciated sights I'd ever laid eyes on! Their presence transported me from absolute terror to complete security. I knew nothing bad would happen now that they were watching over me.

> Aside from Jesus and the police, whom are you most likely to call on when you're scared? Why does this person make you feel safe?

All but giddy with gratitude, I eventually noticed that none of my new heroes had their guns drawn, and one of them even seemed to be suppressing a smile. I turned to see what he was looking at and was surprised to see Sheriff Long walking toward me. That's when they broke the news that I'd just called 911 on the lawman, who had graciously dropped by to check on me. My first emergency-services request, and I'd almost gotten the big guy riddled with holes!

While I'm still totally embarrassed by my blunder, I'm glad to have firsthand experience of how capable our sheriff's department is. I may live in a village that resembles Mayberry, but there aren't any Barney Fifes sporting a badge around here! Our law-enforcement officers mean business. They serve with bravery and competence. Having them in charge of Williamson County makes me feel safe.

Which reminds me of the implied message of the next psalm we're going to peruse: we are guaranteed safety and security because our Savior reigns over the whole world! Plus, we don't need to hide when God knocks at the door, misunderstanding His intentions; we can be absolutely certain that *everything* He does is for our good and His glory.

THEY'RE PLAYING OUR SONG...MOST OF THE TIME

Whenever I see an unflattering picture of Kirstie Alley wearing sweatpants and eating ice cream in *People* magazine, I can relate. Comfortable outfits and sugar cravings are definitely within the realm of my experience. But when I see a photo of Katie Holmes immaculately dressed and perfectly posed on the cover of *In Style,* I have absolutely no frame of reference. I've never worn a size 2 or had millions of dollars in disposable income!

From my perspective the vast majority of the 150 psalms are more Kirstie than Katie. They pretty much read like a scrapbook of my life, with days of delight and dancing followed by days of disappointment and regret. Even most of the ones labeled "royal" or "Messianic" include a few elements that mirror the ups and downs of our lives. For instance, some of Psalm 22 (one of the most familiar psalms that includes prophetic imagery about Jesus) reads like a play-by-play of the crucifixion—most notably verses 14–18. Yet a lot of the situations described in Psalm 22 were literally experienced by King David; he could relate!

However, the message of Psalm 110—which the nineteenth-century preacher Charles Spurgeon described as "the crown of all the Psalms"[1] and which is the psalm most often quoted in the New Testament[2]—doesn't have any application to David or other earthly kings. This petite psalm clearly describes a conversation that could only take place between God the Father and God the Son, between Yahweh and Adonai.

In fact, David makes it obvious from the very beginning that he isn't talking about himself:

> The LORD says to my Lord:
>   "Sit at my right hand,
> until I make your enemies your footstool."
>   *Psalm 110:1*

David could not have written this song from personal experience because he wouldn't have called his heirs "Lord." He might've called Solomon—the academic stud who aced the SAT, grew into a ladies' man, and became the third king of Israel—"Mr. Smarty-Pants." Or he might've called Absalom a "spoiled brat," given the hottie's obsession with expensive hair products and his lust for power. But he certainly wouldn't have called either one of them "Lord."

What's more, if you'll flip a few inches to the right in your Bible to the book of Hebrews, you'll see this same footstool allegory used to describe Jesus:

> And every priest stands daily at his service, offering repeatedly the same sacrifices, which can never take away sins. But when Christ had offered for all time a single sacrifice for sins, he sat down at the right hand of God, waiting from that time until his enemies should be made a footstool for his feet. *Hebrews 10:11–13*

That means Psalm 110 isn't a Kirstie tune. You won't be tempted to write a similar song in your diary or find yourself thinking, *Wow, I can totally relate to this passage,* unless you're a pathological narcissist! In contrast to the familiar emotions that fill much of the Psalter, David is describing a situation that's outside the realm of our experience.

> **PSALMS: THE INSIDE STORY**
> Some modern theologians teach that, in a sense, all psalms are Messianic because they all "anticipate the Messiah."[3]

He is anticipating that moment in history when God exalts Jesus to His rightful position as ruler of all, when the Father invites His only begotten Boy to hang out in heaven until the wicked become an ottoman for Immanuel to rest His Birkenstocks on.

BOTH A PRINCE AND A PRIEST

After clearly identifying Jesus as the leading man in this story, David gushes about His wielding a scepter and governing the world and ruling over the good guys, who rally to Christ's side in battle (verse 3), *and* the bad guys, who will surely get swatted down by His scepter (verse 2):

> The LORD sends forth from Zion
>> your mighty scepter.
>> Rule in the midst of your enemies!
> Your people will offer themselves freely
>> on the day of your power,
>> in holy garments;
> from the womb of the morning,
>> the dew of your youth will be yours. *Psalm 110:2–3*

But then our Old Testament poet seemingly veers off course by comparing Christ to an obscure high priest with a hard-to-pronounce name:

> The LORD has sworn
>> and will not change his mind,
> "You are a priest forever
>> after the order of Melchizedek." *Psalm 110:4*

Much has been made about this man named Mel and the traits he shares with Jesus. Their common denominators are as follows:

- Mel's royal title, the "king of Salem" (Genesis 14:18), means "king of peace"; Jesus is called the "Prince of Peace" (Isaiah 9:6).
- Mel was also a priest, but he wasn't invited to Levitical family reunions because he wasn't from the tribe of Levi (Hebrews

7:1–10); Jesus wasn't from the tribe of Levi either (Matthew 1:1–17).

- Scripture doesn't specify the end of Mel's reign, therefore it appears timeless; according to Revelation 11:15, our Redeemer Jesus will reign eternally too!

By using Mel as a metaphor in verse 4, David is portraying Jesus as *both* prince and high priest, as our ruler *and* our intercessor. Furthermore,

---

PSALMS: THE INSIDE STORY

When David wrote, "The LORD says," at the beginning of Psalm 110 and, "The LORD has sworn," in verse 4, he was distinguishing these statements from other comments about God and Jesus in the psalm. David's grammatical qualifications establish verses 1 and 4 as oracles—*direct statements* from God. Which is sort of like saying these are the super-duper important points of the song![4]

---

by recording God's proclamation of Christ's "forever" priesthood, Psalm 110 highlights Jesus's superiority over other priests. Although God called the priests to lead His people in worship—and according to biblical history some of them did a good job—they were inherently flawed.

No matter how dedicated, sincere, eloquent, or kind, all human religious leaders are still sinners. They may have a better grasp of weighty theological issues, and those clerical collars make them look distinguished (if not a bit claustrophobic), but they aren't perfect. Their sermons can't save us. Nor can the wine they dispense in fancy goblets, nor the grape juice in plastic thimbles, wash away our mistakes. Plus, all priests, pastors, preachers, and teachers will eventually kick the bucket and turn to dust, just like the rest of us. Only Christ's reign is timeless. Only His perfect love can clean up the mess we've gotten ourselves into.

A GOLDEN CROWN AND FLASHING SWORD

Fueled by holy fervor—and perhaps a touch of testosterone—David concludes Psalm 110 with an epic battle scene:

> The Lord is at your right hand;
>> he will shatter kings on the day of his wrath.
> He will execute judgment among the nations,
>> filling them with corpses;
> he will shatter chiefs
>> over the wide earth.
> He will drink from the brook by the way;
>> therefore he will lift up his head. *Psalm 110:5–7*

PSALMS: THE INSIDE STORY

We mustn't forget David was a soldier before he became a king. Before he even started shaving, he went toe to toe against a brute named Goliath.[5] Long before that—when he was still a little boy—his dad and older brothers surely regaled him with dramatic stories about clashes between the Israelites and other nations. That's probably why we're left with the image of Jesus's pausing to drink from a brook while in pursuit of His enemy, just as David had been told that another Hebrew soldier named Gideon had done generations before.[6]

The warrior imagery in these last three verses reminds me of an incident that took place when I was a little girl riding around town with my dad. There we were, cruising down Sanford Avenue, minding our own business, when a boy in a Mustang zoomed past us with a bad word and an obscene gesture. Dad didn't say anything, but when we got to the next red light, he put the truck in Park, walked over to the surprised offender, and pulled him right out of his snazzy sports car. Then he sort of tossed the trembling teen on the hood and gave him a stern lecture about appropriate behavior. Mr. Cussy-Pants quickly became apologetic, and several drivers who'd observed the confrontation started clapping in response.

I watched everything unfold with saucer eyes and thought to myself, *Wow, you'd better not mess with my dad. He's tough!* In that moment a newfound respect for him welled up in me. He got bigger in my heart and mind.

I can't help but wonder if David's understanding of the Messiah bulged in a similar way when he wrote this psalm. Maybe pondering Jesus wearing iridescent robes, wielding a scepter, and scattering enemies left and right made old David's eyes widen and his mouth drop open as he whispered the word, "Wow!"

While much of the Psalter is about suffering, the language of this celebratory Messianic psalm clearly points to Jesus as our conquering hero!

> ### CARRYING THE WEIGHT OF AUTHORITY
> Each year when Queen Elizabeth II presides over the State Opening of Parliament, she wears the Imperial State Crown—a subtle little accessory set with 2,868 diamonds, 273 pearls, 17 sapphires, 11 emeralds, and 5 rubies.[7] Carried just in front of her as part of the royal procession is the jewel-encrusted Sword of State, which symbolizes the sovereign's royal power and authority.[8] What a fascinating reminder of how our King of kings reigns with unparalleled power and ultimate authority!

WONDERFUL IS RIGHT AROUND THE CORNER

In much the same way my fear of the neighborhood lurker kept me from enjoying pleasant evenings at home for a while, sometimes I lose sight of God's glory because I'm too caught up in the trivial inconveniences of everyday life. A recent trip reminded me of this in a way I won't soon forget.

After almost twenty years of constant air travel, I've become a jaded frequent flier. I don't like having to squeeze shampoo and conditioner and eye-makeup remover into wee bottles to keep from having my carry-on bag confiscated. I don't like having to take off my shoes at security check-in and expose a shoddy pedicure to perfect strangers. And I really don't like wedging into seats configured for a skinny supermodel, only to have some grumpy businessman glare at me because he needs more room. As a result I've digressed to the point of being antisocial on airplanes.

I was in my antisocial posture recently—reading a book with iPod earbuds in and avoiding eye contact with the other passengers—when I noticed a commotion making its way through first class. A little boy about four or five years old was galloping down the aisle, all but dragging an exhausted-looking woman laden with bags. I thought to myself, *Uh-oh, I bet the tiny talker ends up sitting next to me.* Sure enough, he bounced into my row, followed by his mom, who inadvertently whacked me in the head with something hard and pointy. I managed a faint smile, feeling a little compassion for her plight, and then leaned away from her son, hoping she'd already laced his juice box with Dramamine.

No such luck.

It soon became obvious that he was not only having his first flight experience but had inhaled a heavy dose of sugar beforehand. He gyrated in the window seat, peering out the porthole while narrating in detail the action taking place outside the plane. His words increased in speed and volume during our taxi and takeoff until his voice was a shriek audible only to dogs and very exasperated seatmates. But the screeching stopped abruptly once we were in the air.

I thought, *Oh no, he's probably swallowed a peanut.* Glancing over to make sure he was okay, I was graced by the sight of a child completely entranced. His eyes were wide, his mouth was open, and his chubby fists were clasped to his chest. When he recovered his voice and resumed his commentary, I closed my book, leaned back against the headrest, and thoroughly enjoyed listening to him compare clouds to cotton candy.

Seeing his cherubic face illuminated with wonder made me realize I'd become so consumed by the inconveniences of air travel that I'd lost the anticipatory joy of visiting new places or returning to favorite haunts. Of reconnecting with old friends or meeting new ones. I'd forgotten that airports usually represent something to look forward to: families scanning the baggage-claim crowd to find their loved ones at Christmastime or soldiers returning home to meet the babies who were born while they were deployed.

I think that's the biggest benefit of prophetic imagery in the psalms as well; it reminds us we have something to look forward to. It helps us appreciate that life here on this broken planet is not all there is. That the victory of acquiring stainless steel appliances and the defeat of bad hair days is not the sum total of our existence. That something infinitely better awaits us. Because one day—one glorious day—all our trouble and pain will vanish when Jesus splits the sky, riding a white horse with "King of kings and Lord of lords" tattooed on His thigh! And on that day we'll realize His love for us was worth it all.

When I wake up, I will see your likeness and be satisfied.
Psalm 17:15, NCV

⚉ *The right-now relevance of Psalm 110* ⚉

God's love established Jesus as our compassionate Savior *and* conquering Hero, so we can celebrate our redeemed status now and look forward to Christ's ultimate reign in the future.

ENOUGH ABOUT ME. WHAT ABOUT YOU?

1. Read Acts 2:14–36, noting particularly verses 34 and 35. Why do you think Peter used Psalm 110 as Old Testament proof that Jesus was the Messiah in this (his very first) sermon to an audience of religious Jews? What in the psalm explicitly points to Jesus?

2. Read Psalm 22. This psalm is often used as an example of a Messianic psalm because Jesus uttered the first verse while suffering on the cross (see Matthew 27:46; Mark 15:34). It's also quoted from or alluded to several other times in the New Testament. What images in Psalm 22 strike you as most distinctly Christlike and/or crosslike?

3. How would you describe the difference, if any, between God's intent and the individual songwriters' intent with regards to the psalms?

4. Read Psalms 51:10; 104:30; and 139:7–8. These passages reveal that, just like Jesus, the Holy Spirit is also an integral part of Old Testament theology. What adjectives come to mind when you consider the active presence of this third member of the Trinity in Psalms?

5. How can truths from the Old Testament affect our lives in these New Testament times?

6. What specific things or relationships are most likely to distract you from looking forward to being with Jesus?

8

PROJECT OF A LIFETIME

What Psalm 8 says about God's partnering

with imperfect people like us

In those days the church was not merely a thermometer
that recorded the ideas and principles of popular opinion;
it was a thermostat that transformed the mores of society.
—MARTIN LUTHER KING JR.

Out of all the summer jobs I had during high school and college, my absolute favorite was being a lifeguard, ski instructor, and group leader at a Christian camp near Gainesville, Florida. I worked there with about twenty other teenagers every summer from ninth grade until my sophomore year in college—and loved every minute of it.

Don't get the wrong idea; this was no glamour job. The ramshackle staff cabins weren't air-conditioned, so it was hot. And the camp was situated in the woods between two lakes, so it was humid and infested with supersized bugs. Plus, our jobs started early in the morning and didn't end until our late-night rounds to make sure the boys weren't running the girl's undergarments up the flagpole or vice versa, so our hourly pay worked out to something like thirty-nine cents! But despite sweltering heat, slave wages, and humongous horse flies, those long days at Lake Swan Camp remain one of the highlights of my life.

I remember being so excited the first summer I was hired that I couldn't stop fidgeting in the car on the way there. I remember watching the cool kids who'd previously worked at camp for cues on how to act during our first staff-orientation meeting. I remember how they all sat up straight and got quiet when the camp director, Mr. Rollins, walked into the room. I remember listening attentively as he told us that for the next three months we'd be ambassadors for Lake Swan Camp and, more important, ambassadors for Jesus Christ. He went on to explain how he expected us to behave as Christian leaders: to be honest and kind and to work hard. Just before closing in prayer, he spoke with an inspirational flourish about how he was entrusting us with the ministry God had given him.

That was the first time an adult looked me in the eye and said something along the lines of "I'm leaving you in charge." I soberly realized someone I respected was expecting big things from my fourteen-year-old self.

Of course I never had to manage emergencies on my own. When a little boy was stung by a bee on the beach and went into anaphylactic shock while I was on lifeguard duty, Tim Rollins (the director's younger brother) swooped in from seemingly out of nowhere and carried him to the infirmary for life-saving treatment. When our teammate Craig was bitten on the finger by a pygmy rattlesnake while clearing brush, the director rushed him to the hospital in Gainesville while the associate director corralled us into the chapel to pray. (Craig recovered fully and didn't lose the wounded digit as was direly predicted by the ER doc who admitted him.) And when we counseled with younger kids in chapel, a youth pastor was typically hovering nearby just in case we got in over our heads and needed him to chime in.

> Describe the job (not necessarily for pay) that most nearly stretched you to the limit of your abilities. Were you initially hesitant and intimidated, or were you raring to go and excited about the challenge?

Although I knew someone older and wiser would come alongside if I needed help, I still sometimes felt like a toddler in water wings who'd been thrown into the deep end of the pool! I learned that when somebody in authority hands you the keys to his kingdom and says, "Govern well," it's both an affirmation of your gifts and a forewarning of much more responsibility.

Delegating the activities of a Christian camp to a bunch of adolescents in mildewed bathing suits is not unlike God graciously allowing mankind to supervise this spinning orb called Earth. It's an exciting challenge but also an intimidating proposition. It's exciting because it's as if our heavenly Father has handed us the keys to His classic car; it's intimidating because we might just wrap the priceless vehicle around a tree!

STINKERS MINDING GOD'S STORE

Psalm 8 describes the assignment God has given mankind to preside over our planet. This psalm has been informally titled "The Crown of Creation,"[1] and believe it or not, you and I are the glittering tiara in the metaphor! Lest we become haughty in light of our exalted role, David starts his ode to earthly influence by comparing us to babies:

> O LORD, our Lord, your majestic name fills the earth!
> Your glory is higher than the heavens.
>
> You have taught children and infants
> to tell of your strength,
> silencing your enemies
> and all who oppose you. *Psalm 8:1–2, NLT*

These first two verses reveal that not only does everything *above* the earth sing God's praises, but He's so powerful that even the cries of the weakest *on* the earth (infants and children) can hush His detractors. God's magnificence is so unmistakable it doesn't take an eloquent orator to defend it.

David continues this theme by musing about what a miracle it is that the Creator of the universe even gives puny people like us the time of day:

> When I look at the night sky and see the work
>> of your fingers—
> the moon and the stars you set in place—
> what are mere mortals that you should think about them,
>> human beings that you should care for them?
>> *Psalm 8:3–4, NLT*

We find a similar question in Psalm 144:3–4, where the writer points out the brevity of life. Job, too, says something along these lines as a way of crying uncle after being hit by wave after wave of suffering (see 7:7). But when David asks, "What are mere mortals that you should think about them?" we hear no hint of sarcasm or despair. Instead our ancient hymn writer sounds like a little boy looking up at his favorite sports hero in wide-eyed wonder. David's query is laced with genuine astonishment: *How can a perfect God like Him love messy people like us?*

Psalm 8:3–4 reminds me of one the few Latin phrases I remember

---

PSALMS: THE INSIDE STORY

The phrase "When I look at your heavens, the work of your fingers" in Psalm 8 (ESV) is an anthropomorphism, which is a fancy, multisyllabic term for attributing human characteristics or behavior to nonhuman things like God or cartoon animals. David didn't know whether God has literal fingers or not; he chose the poetic imagery of "the work of your fingers" to emphasize how even the magnitude of creation is miniaturized by the omnipresence of God.

---

from seminary: *simul justus et peccator,* which means "simultaneously righteous and sinful." We're justified because of God's great mercy, but we're also guilty because of our inherent unrighteousness. We are both saints and sinners. Sanctified stinkers. As such we should demonstrate the healthy duality of acknowledging our depravity and being awed by God's love and forgiveness.

YOU LOOK A LITTLE LIKE YOUR FATHER

I'm guessing that after the self-effacing qualification of verses 3 and 4, a shy smile lit up David's countenance. Because surely he was thinking how glad he was to be a *redeemed* ratfink as he continued writing:

> Yet you made them only a little lower than God
> > and crowned them with glory and honor.
> You gave them charge of everything you made,
> > putting all things under their authority—
> the flocks and the herds
> > and all the wild animals,
> the birds in the sky, the fish in the sea,
> > and everything that swims the ocean currents.
> > *Psalm 8:5–8, NLT*

Talk about taking a risk! This passage declares that God put us in charge. He's given the Office of Earth Management to messy people. He's handed prodigals His power of attorney. It's hard to believe the Lord's optimistic assignment isn't a typo, but David's song actually harks back to the beginning of recorded biblical history when God first gave humans His stamp of approval:

> Then God said, "Let us make man in our image, after our like-
> ness. And let them have dominion over the fish of the sea and
> over the birds of the heavens and over the livestock and over all

the earth and over every creeping thing that creeps on the earth."

> So God created man in his own image,
>> in the image of God he created him;
>> male and female he created them.

> And God blessed them. And God said to them, "Be fruitful and multiply and fill the earth and subdue it and have dominion over the fish of the sea and over the birds of the heavens and over every living thing that moves on the earth." *Genesis 1:26–28*

It's important to note that when God said, "Be fruitful and multiply," He wasn't simply encouraging couples to frolic and make babies. God was commanding His people to fill the world with His glory, because as His image-bearers we reflect a glimmer of who He is. Even the whiniest, most colicky newborns bring a flicker of the divine into our unfolding drama, because they bear God's thumbprint! And we grownups reflect God's glory in everyday ways as well, no matter what our bathroom mirrors suggest.

When the Alpha and Omega sanctioned our place as the crown of creation, it was both an expression of His favor and a symbol of the huge responsibility humans have been given. We're called to echo our heavenly Father's persona and exercise authority on His behalf. And since we are made *like God*, we are created to reveal what *God is like*. Our Creator-Redeemer plopped us on this planet—large and in charge—to reflect His character, to play a small role in redeeming all that's broken in our world.

We can do that in several ways:

- Expressing compassion rather than criticism or indifference. That could mean listening to your mother-in-law's monologue about her recent doctor's appointment instead of screening your calls.

- Leading others by humbling ourselves. That could mean offering your help to an overwhelmed co-worker or small-group leader.

- Reflecting God's grace in routine tasks. That could mean scraping Cheerios off the breakfast table with a smile or playing yet another tedious round of Candy Land with your little ones without complaining.

- Realizing that having dominion over nature involves caretaking and stewardship—in other words, recognizing that Christians don't have a hall pass to be unconscionable consumers. That could mean saying no to that cute pair of shoes you don't really need or starting a recycling center in your church. It definitely means no more pitching McDonald's wrappers out the car window!

ONE LAST TRIUMPHANT TOOT OF GOD'S HORN

David ends Psalm 8 with a poetic device called an *inclusio,* which means "beginning and ending a literary unit with essentially the same words."[2]

> O LORD, our Lord, your majestic name fills the earth!
> *Psalm 8:9, NLT*

The general application of this psalm is the divinely delegated authority and responsibility we have as God's image-bearers. But in this final note, David brings us back to the overarching theme of every song in the Psalter, which is to *give praise to God.* To recognize that God—and only God—is the true monarch of all He has made. While our heavenly Father graciously lets us sit in His lap and steer, we must never delude ourselves into thinking we can drive all by ourselves.

I recently heard a sermon about a little-known hero of the faith named Thomas Chalmers, a great leader who started out as a great big boor. He was born in 1780 in the small fishing community of Anstruther, Scotland. He grew up in a relatively poor family in which academics were highly valued. And before most children have mastered potty training, wee Master Chalmers's brilliance had bobbed to the surface. By the age of three, he could read in English, Greek, and Hebrew. By the age of ten, he'd read every single book in the village where he lived with his mom, dad, and thirteen brothers and sisters!

Long before puberty, Thomas Chalmers was packed off to St. Andrews University. He finished his studies—earning advanced degrees in mathematics and theology—by age nineteen. And by the time he was twenty, he was hired to be both a math professor at St. Andrews and the pastor of a small parish.

Some would argue that the mental aptitude of a man like Chalmers is as rare as a happy skinny woman (I'm convinced grumpiness is often linked to a lack of carbohydrates). However, the enormity of his cognitive IQ stood in stark contrast to his underdeveloped heart. Despite his intellect he didn't "get" grace. He acted more like a jerk than like Jesus. He came across as arrogant and condescending and much more interested in ideas than individuals. One of my pastors (George Grant, a studious Chalmers aficionado) says that during this stage of his life, "He was widely admired but universally disliked!"

Thus, God gave young Tom a providential time-out. After witnessing the premature deaths of two siblings from tuberculosis, he fell quite sick himself. He was bedridden for months and came close to kicking the proverbial bucket. But in that weakened physical condition, this gifted young man finally fell in love with his Savior. He realized that in his obsessive quest for knowledge about God and His creation, he'd forfeited an intimate relationship with the Lover of his soul. And once he turned his attention to the heavenly Father's unmerited kindness, he became a totally different man.

When he recovered his physical health, Chalmers resigned from his distinguished university position in order to pour himself into his rural community. He spent several days every week walking the countryside to visit people, whether they attended his church or not! His life became riddled with the language of love. By the time of his death in 1847, Thomas Chalmers had pioneered a vast and effective outreach to the poor and underprivileged, had helped build and pay for at least five hundred new churches, had initiated the construction and funding of more than four hundred new schools, and had trained and deployed over eight hundred missionaries to foreign lands.

Thomas Chalmers lived the latter part of his life in a way that helped redeem his culture. He taught about the

THE POWER OF ONE

As busy as your life is, you can find small ways to make a big difference. Check out some of the following Web sites for ideas:

- www.compassion.com: Learn how sponsoring a child through Compassion International can help break the cycle of poverty.
- www.heifer.org: Find ideas for giving families a source of food and income to foster self-reliance and hope.
- www.feedingamerica.org: Discover opportunities in your local community for aiding in the efforts of this national food-bank network.
- www.volunteermatch.org: Type in your zip code to get a list of local opportunities where you can put your passion into action.

Bread of Life from the pulpit and handed out literal bread from soup kitchens. He worshiped God in sanctuaries and on street corners, with passion and practicality. His compassionate sociology reflected his Christ-centered theology. He fulfilled God's mission of dominion by loving and serving the people around him. Which is the key to living out the lyrics of Psalm 8.

BULLIES BEWARE

Sometimes when I think about the sorry state of our world, I feel about as inadequate as I did that first summer at Lake Swan Camp when I initially felt the burden of being responsible for others. The appalling smut passed off as entertainment, the horror of women and children sold for their bodies, the uncertainty of how best to care for the planet—I can't decide whether to build a bunker in the backyard or race out in full battle regalia. Perhaps you too have felt overwhelmed by the sight of hungry faces on the evening news or have been moved to anger by the casual attitude others have toward God's gift of life.

The good news is that a little bit of elbow grease on our part goes a long way when coupled with our heavenly Father's compassion for humanity. Just a smidgen of love will often sweeten a bitter relationship. A morsel of mercy can soften the most callous criminal. And a teaspoon of biblical truth, seasoned with grace, has the power to enlighten those who've been duped.

We must not forget that when God handed mankind the authority to manage His creation, He didn't intend for us to govern with an iron fist. We won't change society for good through autocratic bullying, scowling in disapproval, or waving protest placards. Instead we can permeate our world with God's glory by engaging our culture in much the same way Thomas Chalmers did. By sharing microwave popcorn with a Muslim co-worker; by voluntarily cleaning up an abandoned lot in town; by chatting with the lonely, blue-haired ladies in church; or by simply dropping off a casserole to a frazzled single mom who works two jobs to support her family.

We will lead the way God intended when we love well the other messy image-bearers He weaves into our stories.

== *The right-now relevance of Psalm 8* *==*

God's love frees us from self-centeredness so we can take on worthwhile responsibilities that can be accomplished only through His strength and wisdom.

ENOUGH ABOUT ME. WHAT ABOUT YOU?

1. Who's the most Christlike boss you've ever had? Describe one or two positive imprints his or her leadership left on your heart.

2. Someone once observed, "God made man in His own image, and then man returned the compliment."[3] In the arena of leadership, how do you think Christians most often distort God's image?

3. Read Mark 9:33–35 and Matthew 18:2–5. What boundaries do these New Testament teachings of Jesus draw around the mandates we find in Genesis 1:26–28 and Psalm 8:5–9?

4. In light of our divine appointment as "planet managers," how do you think Christians should respond to global concerns like pollution, energy conservation, and ozone depletion?

5. Reread Psalm 8:1–2, 9, and then read Luke 10:19–20. What human calling ranks above our having dominion over nature? How would your approach to others change if you stopped to remember your own state as a sanctified stinker?

6. Set a date with some friends or family to rent and watch the movie *Amazing Grace,* which details William Wilberforce's crusade to abolish slavery. Afterward loiter over coffee and dessert to discuss what you could do to promote social justice in your corner of the world and in so doing to glorify God.

9

THE ART OF APPRECIATION

What Psalm 34 reveals about being grateful

for God's ability to unsnarl the tangles in our lives

The psalms wonderfully solve the problem
of a praise-deficient culture
by providing the necessary words.
—PHILIP YANCEY

About ten years ago, when I was on staff at Focus on the Family, I had the privilege of overseeing and emceeing their national women's conference series Renewing the Heart. We held events in coliseums around the country, and it was amazing to watch as many as twenty thousand women worshiping God in venues that had featured professional wrestling matches the weekend before! Of course, it was also an ongoing challenge to put together a schedule with just the right amount of serious Bible teaching and sensory entertainment. In response to that programming goal, I came up with the bright idea of rappelling from the rafters of the auditorium to the stage following the lunch break. I reasoned it was the time of day when conference attendees tend to get sleepy and distracted. Plus I thought it'd be a fun way to demonstrate that being a Christian doesn't mean you have to be boring!

Initially Dr. Dobson and the rest of the leadership team resisted my idea. In addition to liability issues, they were concerned that I might fall to my death in front of an innocent crowd. But I assured them about the safety of the stunt—especially in light of my previous mountain-climbing experience—and eventually they gave their grudging consent.

It wasn't until right before my debut descent at the Greensboro Coliseum in North Carolina that I began to have second thoughts. I hadn't

considered until then that it would be a free fall, that unlike when I'd rap-
pelled in the Rockies, I'd have nothing but air underneath my feet on the
way down. As I followed Jerry (the crewman directing the details of my
daredevil stunt) up a rickety metal ladder and onto a catwalk eighty feet
above the oblivious crowd, I started sweating like a sumo wrestler in a
sauna. When I looked down, my stomach started doing backflips, and I
found myself thinking, *Those ladies wouldn't like it very much if I got
physically sick right about now!*

After ten or fifteen minutes of anxious waiting in that precarious
perch, I heard the worship team begin to sing "I'll Fly Away," which was
my cue to unhook the safety line from my harness and plummet toward
the concrete floor. I'd probably still be cowering in the attic of the Greensboro Coliseum if sweet Jerry hadn't given me a thumbs-up, along with a
promise to control the descent speed himself. When the cameras panned
to me zooming down from the pinnacle of the arena while grinning and waving, the audience applauded wildly. They didn't know my wide smile was a thin disguise for terror!

> What's the most recent circumstance that caused you to feel over-whelming gratitude toward God?

Absolute relief rushed through me when my feet finally landed on terra firma. I was so happy to be standing on solid ground, I
wanted to bend down and kiss it! Immeasurably thankful for God's pro-
tection in spite of my stupidity, I couldn't help whispering, "Thank You,
Jesus…thank You, Jesus" over and over again. Overwhelming gratitude
strained the seams of my heart.

A comparable sentiment of seam-busting thanksgiving reverberates
through many of the psalms. Because, like us, the psalmists were constantly getting themselves into precarious situations and in desperate need
of God's help—and He always came through when they found themselves in trouble and cried out for His mercy!

CRAZY OVER GOD'S COMPASSION

My dog Harley gets so excited when I give him a barbecued pig's ear (yes, they're as gross as they sound, but my dogs adore them) that he jumps straight up into the air like a jack-in-the-box. His gratitude for the gift of severed pork parts triggers a hilarious *boing* effect. And he wears a sort of dopey doggy grin the whole time he's bouncing!

David's appreciation for God's grace at the beginning of Psalm 34 is so enthusiastic that he seems to be bouncing and smiling too:

> I will bless the LORD at all times;
>> his praise shall continually be in my mouth.
> My soul makes its boast in the LORD;
>> let the humble hear and be glad.
> Oh, magnify the LORD with me,
>> and let us exalt his name together! *Psalm 34:1–3*

PSALMS: THE INSIDE STORY

Psalm 34 is an acrostic, which means the first word in each verse begins with the successive letter from the twenty-two letters in the Hebrew alphabet (with the exception of the last verse, which should technically correspond to the last letter in the Hebrew alphabet, *waw*).[1] Acrostic poems were commonly used in ancient Jewish literature as a way of helping readers memorize the text. The passage in Proverbs 31 about the woman who was like Martha Stewart, Rachel Ray, and Beth Moore rolled into one is another example of acrostic poetry!

The phrase "at all times" in verse 1 is better translated "at every time,"[2] which is noteworthy in light of the circumstances connected to these lyrics. According to the official canonical title[3] of Psalm 34, David crafted these words immediately after feigning insanity to escape from a cruel Philistine king named Achish[4] (also known as Abimelech).

The story behind his "wild-'n'-crazy guy" act is that he was not only standing in front of an enemy king, but he was doing so while holding Goliath's sword.[5] Remember, Goliath was the behemoth star of the Philistine army until David killed him with a stone from a slingshot and then beheaded him with his own blade in front of his entire platoon. A modern parallel would be if an American Green Beret who had personally killed Osama bin Laden found himself standing in front of the head of al Qaeda. So David didn't compose this song while dancing around in a meadow with a harp, nor was he expressing superficial gratitude about getting to enjoy an extra cup of java before tending sheep. Instead he was pouring out praise at the end of what surely must have been a very stressful day.

No Shame in Slobbering

And this scriptural thank-you note takes on even more significance when you read between the lines of the next passage:

> I sought the LORD, and he answered me
> and delivered me from all my fears.
> Those who look to him are radiant,
> and their faces shall never be ashamed.
> This poor man cried, and the LORD heard him
> and saved him out of all his troubles.

The angel of the LORD encamps

around those who fear him, and delivers them.

Psalm 34:4–7

Did you notice the point David makes about people who trust in God never having to be ashamed (verse 5)? Well, the biblical account of his confrontation with Achish describes David as "drooling down his beard" as part of his pretense of lunacy (1 Samuel 21:13, NLT). Now having spit in your facial hair was an embarrassing no-no in ancient Eastern culture.[6] No self-respecting man would dribble in his whiskers. Yet there he was—a Jewish hero for having killed the Philistine Goliath, slobbering in front of a Philistine king. How utterly humiliating for David. He must've hated acting like a nut in front of foreign enemies who undoubtedly had his picture plastered all over their post offices.

I find it amazing that, in the aftermath of that degradation, David managed to craft this joy-filled psalm. His underlying message is that even if your story includes a humiliating chapter—and all of ours do—God's people don't ever have to walk in shame. Those embarrassing memories that still make your stomach muscles clench, like when you suddenly realized the slowpoke you were honking at was your pastor or when your child blurted out an insulting comment about a fellow grocery shopper or when your husband found out you had an abortion in college—all are covered by God's merciful forgiveness. We can hold our heads high because our heavenly Father will somehow redeem everything.

CONTAGIOUS GRATITUDE

Next David shifts from sharing his personal testimony to urging others to have firsthand experience with God:

Oh, taste and see that the LORD is good!
   Blessed is the man who takes refuge in
      him!
Oh, fear the LORD, you his saints,
   for those who fear him have no lack!
The young lions suffer want and hunger;
   but those who seek the LORD lack no good
      thing. *Psalm 34:8–10*

Have you ever turned to a friend while enjoying a great meal and said, "You just have to taste this"? I've done this many times, most recently in a little Italian restaurant in New York. I was savoring some of the best tiramisu that has ever crossed my lips and instinctively knew the people dining with me couldn't begin to appreciate the espresso-soaked nirvana (the literal translation of *tiramisu* is "pick-me-up" because of the yummy combination of sugar and caffeine) unless they sampled it themselves. So I scooped up a decadent gob and shoved the spoon toward my startled neighbor, proclaiming, "You just have to taste this!"

That's the gist of David's dramatic decree in Psalm 34:8–10. He's been so blessed by his relationship with God he can't help encouraging others to get to know Him! If we've tasted sacred grace, we'll have similar evangelistic exuberance too. We'll want others to experience the same unconditional affection that has transformed our messy lives.

I think experiencing God's mercy is kind of like trudging through the desert, near death, and miraculously stumbling upon a bottomless spring of cool, fresh water. Afterward we'd be flagging down every dusty traveler we spotted with the enthusiastic yell, "Hey, there's an oasis over here!"

THE SOWING PRINCIPLE

In the next section of Psalm 34, David changes to a proverb style of communication, thereby offering his listeners practical principles for savoring the full-meal deal in their relationships with God:

> Come, O children, listen to me;
>> I will teach you the fear of the LORD.
> What man is there who desires life
>> and loves many days, that he may see good?
> Keep your tongue from evil
>> and your lips from speaking deceit.
> Turn away from evil and do good;
>> seek peace and pursue it. *Psalm 34:11–14*

Although these verses sound like the beginning of a children's sermon, they're actually addressed to Israel as a whole—to all of God's children, not just the ones in Pull-Ups and pigtails. And David's main point is that if you want to experience the good life, then do life well. The blessings of God are best experienced in doing His will, not in disobedience.

A SUPERNATURAL SENSE OF HEARING

After that short homily on holiness, David resumes his exultation about how we're the objects of God's biased attention:

> The eyes of the LORD are toward the righteous
>> and his ears toward their cry.

> The face of the LORD is against those who do evil,
>> to cut off the memory of them from the earth.
> When the righteous cry for help, the LORD hears
>> and delivers them out of all their troubles.
> The LORD is near to the brokenhearted
>> and saves the crushed in spirit. *Psalm 34:15–18*

I like David's emphasis on our heavenly Father's acute sense of hearing with regard to us; it reminds me of something I observed while visiting one of my mommy friends not too long ago. My dear friend Judy and her tall husband, Tom, welcomed me into their Colorado home shortly after their darling son, Ryan, was born (big sister, Katie, is a keeper too!). I found myself fascinated by the way Judy would pause in the middle of a quiet conversation, turn to Tom, and say, "Honey, will you please go upstairs and check on the baby?" A few minutes later he'd come loping back downstairs to announce Ryan had a dirty diaper or was lying awake in his crib. I didn't hear a peep coming from the nursery, but Judy could hear the faintest murmur from her newborn!

So it is with our divine Dad. God is supernaturally tuned in to our frequency. His blazing eyes take in our slightest stir. His holy ears prick at our softest whisper. Better still, He's in close proximity when we cry. You might not notice Him hovering outside the door to your room as Judy does with Ryan and Katie, but He promises to be near all the same. Not one single tear rolls down your cheek without your Savior's noticing.

FOCUSING ON GOD'S FAITHFULNESS

Once again David's words honestly reflect his experience. He'd been through extremely tough stuff: he'd wrestled with lions, been pursued by a homicidal king named Saul, was betrayed by his own lust, and had suffered isolation in the caves of Engedi, far away from friends and family. Not to mention the setting of this psalm, when he had to swallow his pride and give an Oscar-worthy performance just to fool an opponent into thinking he was too cuckoo to be a threat! Yet in spite of his personal afflictions, David praises God for delivering him:

> Many are the afflictions of the righteous,
>> but the LORD delivers him out of them all.
> He keeps all his bones;
>> not one of them is broken. *Psalm 34:19–20*

One of the sweetest memories from my childhood is hearing my mom sing the hymn "Count Your Blessings" while she washed dishes after dinner. I don't know what it was about being up to her elbows in suds that compelled her to count blessings, but that tune was as regular as the fried fish we had every Sunday. I can still remember chasing fireflies in the front yard while Mom's accompanying soprano wafted through the kitchen window:

> When upon life's billows you are tempest tossed,
> When you are discouraged, thinking all is lost,
> Count your many blessings, name them one by one,
> And it will surprise you what the Lord hath done.
>
> Are you ever burdened with a load of care?
> Does the cross seem heavy you are called to bear?
> Count your many blessings, every doubt will fly,
> And you will be singing as the days go by.

Chorus:

Count your blessings, name them one by one;

Count your blessings, see what God hath done!

Count your blessings, name them one by one;

Count your many blessings, see what God hath done!

What I didn't know then is that she crooned those lines of gratitude with such conviction because of her own afflictions. During a difficult marriage to my dad, she'd taken mood-altering medicine her doctor prescribed for severe depression, medicine that was ultimately taken off the market because of its dangerous side effects. As a result she ended up being placed under psychiatric care against her will. She clung to God's side while nearly drowning in the fear of losing her mind and having my sister and me taken away from her.

I'm now eleven years older than my mom was then, and I still can't imagine how scary it must've been. I wish with all my heart her story didn't include that chapter. I hate imagining her in the middle of it. Yet by God's grace alone, she came out singing, praising Him for delivering her.

A PERFECTLY SAFE HAVEN

I like to imagine David finishing this worship sonnet with his eyes closed and his hands raised as he sang:

> Affliction will slay the wicked,
>   and those who hate the righteous will be condemned.
> The LORD redeems the life of his servants;
>   none of those who take refuge in him will be condemned.

Psalm 34:21–22

When I was in elementary school, I loved to go fishing with my step-father, John Angel. Well, I didn't actually love the angler part; I just liked sucking on Life Savers and hanging out while he trawled for bass! Anyway, most of our fishing dates were tame events, but one time we got trapped on a small island on the far side of Puzzle Lake during a hurricane. The ferocious storm whipped the normally placid St. Johns River into a sea of whitecaps and toppled trees

> **PSALMS: THE INSIDE STORY**
> Some of the psalms are so saturated with the theme of gratitude they're formally classified as thanksgiving psalms!

around us. Yet I felt perfectly safe, huddled in the circle of John's burly arms.

David had certainly endured more than his share of hair-raising storms by the time he penned Psalm 34. He was used to high water and howling winds. But he also knew he could trust in the refuge of God's embrace no matter what raged around him. That's why he overflows with gratitude.

GRATITUDE IMPROVES OUR ATTITUDES

Appreciating God's provision and protection isn't just an Old Testament topic; the theme of continual thanksgiving is speckled throughout the New Testament too. For instance, when the apostle Paul was unjustly incarcerated and had plenty of time on his hands, he wrote several notes to budding believers in church plants. In his "prison letter" addressed to Christians living in Ephesus, Paul reiterated David's theme of having a grateful heart in all things: "And give thanks for everything to God the Father in the name of our Lord Jesus Christ" (Ephesians 5:20, NLT).

Then, while still wearing an orange jumpsuit, Paul counseled his Philippian buddies to always pray in the dialect of gratitude: "Do not be anxious about anything, but in everything, by prayer and petition, with thanksgiving, present your requests to God" (4:6, NIV).

I was reminded recently that being thankful instead of anxious isn't as easy as it sounds. I had gotten up early one morning and was literally typing a Bible verse on my Mac laptop when I heard a heard a strange whirring sound. The screen froze. Then a few minutes later it faded to dull gray with a single blinking icon in the center. The icon depicted a file containing a question mark. I'd never seen that symbol before, and I hope never to do so again.

After several more rounds of turning the computer on and off—which is the extent of my technological therapeutic skill—I surrendered to the realization it needed professional help. Which meant I had to take a shower and change out of my pajamas into something presentable and drive twenty miles to the Apple Store, where I'd have to beg a jaded, condescending, twenty-something genius to help me since I hadn't scheduled an appointment at least two weeks in advance. Ugh. Of course, the bigger issue was the book deadline looming just two days away and the possibility that everything I'd written had been wiped out when the laptop coughed and started playing dead.

On the way to the Apple Store, I contemplated screaming expletives at the top of my lungs or flinging desperate pleas toward heaven like, "God, if You'll fix this so I don't lose everything I've been working on, I'll go on a mission trip to Africa!" But the passage I'd been typing immediately before the computer crashed distracted me from having a hissy fit. I just couldn't stop thinking about the words: "Be cheerful no matter what; pray all the time; thank God no matter what happens. This is the way God wants you who belong to Christ Jesus to live" (1 Thessalonians 5:16–18, MSG).

So I tried it. I turned off the radio and asked God to give me peace. Then I thanked Him for blessing me with the finances to buy a car so I could drive to town (it would have been a really long walk in the rain), for creating brains like Steve Jobs's (I can't imagine having to write a whole book in longhand), for giving me a relatively sound mind (at least I could remember bits and pieces of the stuff I'd pecked on the keyboard), for having a second laptop at my disposal (who knew that poky old machine in the closet would save my literary behind?), and for giving me enough sense to e-mail the first ten chapters to my editor before the fatal hiccup (I probably would've said a bad word or two if I'd lost the entire manuscript).

Before I knew it, I wasn't anxious anymore. Gratitude had transformed my attitude. I decided that whatever diagnosis the Mac gurus gave me, it wouldn't be the end of the world. As it turned out, it was simply the end of my hard drive. Although I lost two years' worth of data, representing hundreds of hours of work, the perspective gained was honestly worth the price.

I don't know what messes are threatening to crash your emotional hard drive this season.

> **THE CIRCLE OF BLESSING**
> According to one researcher's ongoing study, "Grateful people report higher levels of positive emotions, life satisfaction, vitality, optimism and lower levels of depression and stress."[7] What's not to be thankful for in that?

Maybe you're worried about your family's financial future because your 401(k) has dwindled to pocket change; maybe you're embroiled in a bitter custody dispute after a stormy divorce; maybe the doctor just informed you the lump in your breast is malignant.

Whatever your circumstances, the galvanizing truth of God's Word is that nothing can change the ending of the supernatural story we've been written into. *Nothing* can separate us from the love of God. Which gives us much to be thankful for —no matter what's going on in our little corner of life's coliseum. And which also means we don't have to wait until we're sure of a safe landing before we start expressing our thankfulness.

━ *The right-now relevance of Psalm 34* ━

God's love frees us from our fears so we can live with thankfulness and peace, even amid the roughest storms.

ENOUGH ABOUT ME. WHAT ABOUT YOU?

1. Describe the top five things (not individuals) you're thankful for right now.

2. What's your favorite movie scene depicting a character overwhelmed with gratitude?

3. If you were writing God a thank-you note, knowing that He'd pay attention to every word, what would be the first and last lines?

4. Reread Psalm 34 and then read Psalm 56. The second psalm is considered the darker version of Psalm 34, because it was also

written by David after his escape from Achish. Which song do you resonate with more, and why?

5. Thanksgiving psalms (such as Psalms 34, 66, 92, 107, 116, and 138) can usually be identified by how they recall a lament God has answered. In other words, the psalmist says something like, "Whew, that was a close one. I'm so glad God rescued me!" Where do you observe that kind of emotion in Psalm 107?

6. Describe a situation when you experienced God's hovering like a loving parent (much the way Judy was so alert to Ryan), clearly in tune with your exact needs.

10

Frantic Isn't a Spiritual Fruit

What Psalm 23 illustrates about how

our Shepherd compels stubborn sheep to rest

Quiet minds, which are established in stillness,
refuse to be perplexed or intimidated.
—Tim Hansel

An old friend and a new friend came over for a visit this past weekend. After noticing the red swing hand painted with the reminder "All Is Well," the comfy rocking chairs on the deck, and the green and white hammock suspended between two trees, my new friend, Linda, commented, "Wow, Lisa, you must be really good at relaxing." At which my old friend, Priscilla, who knows my default setting is typically turned to Fast, burst out laughing! I explained to my confused guest that the swing, rocking chairs, and hammock were actually more like props *reminding* me to rest. Because, regrettably, I'm more of a Martha than a Mary.

> As they continued their travel, Jesus entered a village. A woman by the name of Martha welcomed him and made him feel quite at home. She had a sister, Mary, who sat before the Master, hanging on every word he said. But Martha was pulled away by all she had to do in the kitchen. Later, she stepped in, interrupting them. "Master, don't you care that my sister has abandoned the kitchen to me? Tell her to lend me a hand." *Luke 10:38–40,* MSG

Mary was able to set aside her to-do list long enough to sit at Jesus's feet and focus on Him. But her manic sister, Martha, was too worried about table settings to be still and give Him her full attention. She's the type of chick you could count on for a casserole, yet you wouldn't choose to hang

> Would your friends be more likely to describe you as a Martha or a Mary? Why?

out with her at Starbucks. You just know she'd be so preoccupied scanning the room for health-code violations that she wouldn't hear your heart. Martha had the spiritual handicap of *busyness.* Mary had the God-honoring gift of *being.*

In my experience Christian women tend to emphasize the "go out and do" passages of Scripture more than the "be still and know" parts. We wear our stress like a badge of honor, as if all our activity "on God's behalf" is adding up like frequent-flier miles. And the busiest beavers in church are often labeled the best—until their exhaustion begets disenchantment and they limp away seeking a less-demanding water hole. Sadly, some of the most jaded and emotionally spent people I know got that way from being overly committed to Christian causes.

DON'T DO SOMETHING; JUST STAND THERE

Thankfully our heavenly Father doesn't expect His daughters to burn the candle at both ends. In fact, one of the most beloved hymns in the Psalter makes it clear that God doesn't regard being frantic as a spiritual fruit!

> The LORD is my shepherd; I shall not want. *Psalm 23:1*

I find Psalm 23 especially reassuring because it comes immediately after Psalm 22, where we read the heartrending question, "My God, my God, why have you forsaken me?" (Psalm 22:1). Just as my messy self is prone to do, David goes from feeling utterly abandoned to feeling completely secure in a literary minute! I also think it's interesting that prior to this psalm David has used relatively impersonal terms like *King* or *deliverer* to describe God. Yet now he employs the metaphor *shepherd,* which suggests a much more intimate relationship with Yahweh.

And David is speaking from experience, because he spent his youth tending the flock of his father, Jesse.[1] He'd guided them up mountain trails to the best grasslands and down steep gullies to cool water; he'd rescued stragglers from precarious cliffs and sung soothing melodies to the females while they were giving birth. He'd spent many long nights under the stars, keeping watch, and walked countless miles while carrying newborn lambs across his shoulders. He'd even tangled with a lion and a bear to protect his woolly dependents.[2] David knew firsthand that sheep are utterly reliant on their shepherd for protection and provision. So when he uses the word *shepherd* in this opening lyric, he's emphasizing both our desperate need for God and His attentive care for us.

Then our poetic sheep wrangler takes a deep breath and sings this memorable line:

> He makes me lie down in green pastures.
> He leads me beside still waters. *Psalm 23:2*

Frankly, I think most people of faith caricature our Good Shepherd. My pastor, Scotty Smith, and I were brainstorming about Psalm 23, and he noted how people read it and then mistakenly imagine Jesus to be like a male Breck Girl. Breck Girls were beautiful women with luxurious hair who were featured in an extensive ad campaign for Breck shampoo. This long-running ode to ideal feminine beauty, which included models like Cybill Shepherd, Kim Basinger, and Brooke Shields, is now commemorated at the Smithsonian National Museum of American History.

However, the imagery in this psalm doesn't depict our Redeemer as some wimpy male model with Birkenstocks and hair extensions. On the contrary, even in the scene most evocative of a literal shepherd (verse 2), Jesus grabs us by our metaphorical collars and plops us down in the meadow on our bottoms. He *makes* us rest!

> ### REST'S UNEXPECTED BENEFIT
> Research shows a clear link between sleep deprivation and weight problems. Adults who sleep less than six hours a night have a significantly higher rate of obesity than those who sleep seven to eight hours.[3]

Just as literal shepherds sometimes corral their herds into safe places to protect them from predators and their own stupidity (many a lamb has wandered off to its demise), so the Good Shepherd often compels us to take a break from busyness for our good. Sometimes He nudges us into a nap through the Holy Spirit's conviction. For instance, when you hear the verse "Be *still*, and know that I am God" (Psalm 46:10, emphasis added) over and over again in Bible study and church, then see it magnetized to your friend's refrigerator, it's probably a divine clue to slow down. Sometimes God is even more direct, like when He commanded the Israelites to put to death anyone who refused to rest on the Sabbath (see Exodus 31:12–17). Yikes. Can you imagine if that Old Testament rule was still enforced today? Most of us would be six feet under, pushing up daisies! I'm so glad Jesus freed us from living by the letter of the law; however, we need to remember that the spirit of rest is still very much a part of God's plan for us.

THE PERILS OF NOT PAUSING

The most sober object lesson I've ever had on the importance of rest took place more than a decade of Decembers ago, when some co-workers and I were heading to a leadership conference in Aspen. While it was technically a work event, we were still excited about being freed from our cubicles and hanging out together. A gentle giant named Jim Davis and I volunteered to be the designated drivers because our four-wheel-drive SUVs were less likely to slide on Colorado's snow-packed pavement. So after loading our vehicles down with suitcases, sodas, and snacks, we began our road trip with giggles and caffeinated glee.

The first few hours flew by as we told stories and listened to music. However, a few minutes after we passed the ski town of Vail on Interstate 70, I started pumping the brakes because something huge loomed ahead. Initially I thought it was an elk or a moose, but as our two-car convoy rolled closer, I realized it was much larger than a wild animal; an eighteen-wheeler was sprawled across the highway with smoke billowing from the engine.

Jim and I jerked our vehicles over to the shoulder of the road. He jumped out, yelling for me to get someone to stop oncoming traffic, have someone else call 911, and make sure everybody else stayed put until he found out what was going on. I followed his instructions, then jogged toward the cab of the big rig to see if I could do something else to help. When I raced up, Jim took a protective step in front of me and said, "You don't need to see this, Lisa." Unfortunately, I'd already spotted the body crumpled a few feet in front of us. I didn't know who it was, but I knew immediately he was dead.

We learned the details after the Colorado Highway Patrol investigated the crash. The deceased driver was a young father who was crazy about his kids. He was also an outdoorsman who enjoyed hunting in the Rocky Mountain wilderness. The night we found him, he was returning home from a hunting trip during which he'd had little or no sleep. That's what dulled his senses and caused him to mistake the westbound lane of I-70 for the eastbound lane. That's what caused him to pull directly into the path of a speeding semi. His lack of rest led to disastrous consequences.

At first glance the terms *busy Christian* and *drowsy daddy* appear innocuous. Neither expression signals cause for alarm. Yet both conditions are potentially dangerous. On icy interstates exhaustion can result in tragic accidents; in communities of faith it can result in severe stress, disillusionment, and eventual burnout. It's no wonder God emphasizes our need for replenishment throughout His Word. Besides Psalm 23 there are multiple other passages regarding the importance of rest, including but not limited to Genesis 1:31–2:3; Exodus 31:12–18; 33:12–14; Leviticus 23:3; Numbers 10:33; Deuteronomy 12:8–10; Joshua 1:10–13; 2 Samuel 7:1; 1 Chronicles 22:17–18; Isaiah 32:17–18; Jeremiah 31:1–3; Matthew 11:28–29; and Hebrews 4:9–10.

HE LEADS US BECAUSE HE LOVES US

One of the obvious benefits of literal rest is better physical and mental health; getting a good night's sleep is medically proven to be restorative for both our bodies and our minds. Even more beneficial is the kind of rest David's singing about, because spending quiet time with our Redeemer restores our souls:

> He restores my soul.
> He leads me in paths of righteousness
>   for his name's sake. *Psalm 23:3*

While I was at my friend Ann's house the other night, I listened as her nine-year-old daughter lobbied emphatically to stay up later. She whined about how it was summertime and therefore it wasn't fair for her to have to go to bed at nine o'clock. To which Ann replied lovingly but firmly, "Becca, we just got home from a week at the beach, then you immediately went to Atlanta with your dad, and now you're going to vol-

leyball camp every day. You're worn out. I'll let you stay up later this weekend, but tonight you need at least eight hours of sleep, or you're going to
be miserable tomorrow. So go upstairs and put on your pajamas. I'll be up
in a minute to pray with you."

One day Becca will appreciate her mama's determination to do what's
best for her. She'll realize Ann made her lie down because she loves her.
When she grows up, she'll finally understand that her mom decreed a

---

PSALMS: THE INSIDE STORY

The lyrics in Psalm 23 echo the promise of Exodus. For
example, the concept of God as a shepherd depicts the way
He provided for and protected the Israelites while they wandered in the desert. In addition, the Hebrew verb translated
"guide" is used in both Psalm 23:3 (NIV) and Exodus 15:13 to
illustrate God's leading. Finally, the phrase "for his name's
sake" in Psalm 23:3 is the same expression as the one found
in Psalm 106:7–12 that celebrates God's mercy in the context
of the Israelites' escape from Egypt through the Red Sea.[4]

Therefore, David's supreme trust in God is rooted in the
reality of how He directed and ultimately delivered His people from the wilderness. Looking back at God's faithfulness
can help us walk forward in confidence, remembering that
divine precedents will help us persevere in deep, dark valleys!

---

mandatory rest period so her Energizer Bunny–type batteries would be
replenished for the next day.

How much more is our heavenly Father concerned with His children's well-being? And how much more desperately do we need His
promised restoration to recharge the batteries of our weary souls?

THE SECRET TREASURE OF A TOUGH SHEPHERD

After waxing eloquent about pastures and ponds, David shifts to a more solemn note:

> Even though I walk through the valley
>   of the shadow of death,
>   I will fear no evil,
> for you are with me;
>   your rod and your staff,
>   they comfort me. *Psalm 23:4*

This little verse packs a wallop because it implies God's kids will walk through superscary places. Pitch-black places where we can't see our hands in front of our faces. But even in the blackest circumstances—up to and including physical death—our Abba will not desert us. He is our constant companion in peaceful green pastures and pounding-heart, sweaty-palm valleys. Plus He's a formidable bodyguard who carries a big stick. That's why we can tell fear to take a hike!

Because I'm relaxation impaired, I'm definitely drawn to the theme of rest that flows through Psalm 23, but I'm equally encouraged by the theme of our supernatural Shepherd's strength and authority. Author, professor, and theologian Marva Dawn, a leading expert on Psalms, calls this secondary theme "the hidden promise in Psalm 23"[5] and expounds with these words:

> In verse 4, the phrase, "Thy rod and Thy staff, they comfort me," is usually thought of in soft and gentle terms. We like to hear the word *comfort* as if it were meant to make us comfortable. Recently the Navigator's *Daily Walk* Bible-reading program offered this

arresting sentence: "God does not comfort us to make us comfortable, but to make us comforters."

When we read this phrase in Psalm 23, we must remember that the rod was used by the shepherd for beating and smiting— for chastisement. It was a club, not a feather! (And the staff was a pole ending in a crook to grab a sheep by the neck to keep it, perhaps, from falling over a cliff!) The implication is that sometimes sheep need to be dealt with sternly to keep them in the tracks of righteousness.[6]

I remember being taken aback by the appearance of Bedouin shepherds on my first trip to Israel in '98. The Bedouins are a nomadic people still living in Middle East desert regions whose methods of tending sheep and goats haven't changed much since Old Testament times. I was startled because I had subconsciously expected them to resemble the blond-haired, blue-eyed, spa-robe-clad shepherds I'd seen flannelgraphed in Vacation Bible School and immortalized in stained-glass windows. But the Bedouins didn't look anything like I imagined. They're swarthy and sinewy. They have rough skin from the constant sun exposure and stifling heat of the desert. The few I made contact with also had rough personalities from living a hand-to-mouth existence. The lasting impression I have of those modern-day shepherds isn't one of gentleness but of toughness.

While it's certainly appropriate to take a nap or a walk in the park as a result of meditating on Psalm 23, it would also behoove us to stop viewing Jesus through the lens of sentimentality and instead regard Him as a strong shepherd. A caretaker willing to do really rough things to keep His sheep safe and sound, whether that means fighting off predators or snatching us up by the neck when we stubbornly head toward a cliff edge of rebellion.

HEADING FOR HOME

I love the mind-boggling promise of this next verse, the delightful idea of being God's roommate, especially since His refrigerator is stocked with yummy stuff:

> You prepare a table before me
>   in the presence of my enemies;
> you anoint my head with oil;
>   my cup overflows. *Psalm 23:5*

In Old Testament culture, to eat and drink at someone's table didn't mean grabbing a bite and gabbing with your hosts for an hour or two. It was a much bigger deal. Being invited to sit at someone's table often represented the establishment of a covenant,[7] a bond connecting you to each other for life. For instance, when David invited his best friend's crippled son, Mephibosheth, to eat at his table (long after "Bo's" daddy and grand-daddy, Jonathan and Saul, were killed in battle), he was accepting responsibility for Mephibosheth's well-being.[8] Bo didn't just drop by David's house for a barbecue; he came towing a U-Haul!

Furthermore, when David exults here in Psalm 23 about having his noggin slathered with petroleum, he's really saying we're all VIPs at God's buffet bar. In David's culture when someone anointed a dinner companion's head with oil, it symbolized bestowing honor on the greasy guest. Better still, even if we drip a little sauce down our shirts, God won't relegate you or me to the children's table back in the kitchen; He wants us where He can gaze on us with delight as we feast on His generous bounty.

Finally, David tops his own big-shots-at-the-banquet motif by joyfully announcing that we get to live with our Creator-Redeemer forever and ever.

Surely goodness and mercy shall follow me
> all the days of my life,
and I shall dwell in the house of the LORD
> forever. *Psalm 23:6*

We won't just be checking into God's guest room; His house will be our home. And because of our status as the Alpha and Omega's immediate family, goodness and mercy will chase us like a dog chasing a bone. (The literal meaning of the Hebrew word translated as *follow* in verse 6 means to "pursue," not "bring up the rear."[9]) Contrary to popular Christian culture, God doesn't *pressure* us to do more but instead *pursues* us with His blessings until we reach our final resting place with Him in glory.

So in the eternal scheme of things, we have it made big time! We may be messy servants here, but in heaven we're going to be living it up like royalty in the mansion of the King of kings.

BECOMING A LESS-BUSY BEAVER

I arrived home late this past Friday night after being out of the country for several days. I was so tired I dropped my luggage in the kitchen, staggered through the house, and collapsed into bed. I woke up early the next morning, shuffled to the coffee maker, and then sat down wearily on the couch with a mug of big-girl go-go juice and started thinking about everything I needed to accomplish that day.

I needed to unpack, start a load of laundry, then get the boxes of Christmas paraphernalia down from the attic. I was heading out of town again on Monday, so if I didn't decorate this weekend, I might not have time before Christmas to decorate at all. And since I'd be outside nailing garland on the fence and hanging wreaths, I thought it would be a good idea to go ahead and work on my wilted gardens that really needed to be pruned, mulched, and prepared for winter. Oh, and then there were the dusty hardwood floors that should be mopped and the stack of e-mails filling up my in-box and bills to pay and dogs to feed and calls to return. Whew! Before I'd even gotten out of my pajamas, I was completely overwhelmed.

But then I felt God gently nudge my heart. He whispered, *Pssst, how about just hanging out with Me today?* So I did. I ignored the bulging suitcases. I decided the house would just have to look like Scrooge's this year. I remembered there are great plant sales each spring, so I can always replace those that die this winter. I reasoned that one or two late fees on delinquent bills weren't going to ruin my credit score. With a happy sigh I got up and refilled my coffee cup, lit a crackling fire in the fireplace, and put on my favorite slippers. And I proceeded to have the most wonderful day doing nothing except being with my heavenly Father.

If you're like me and identify more with Martha than Mary, I hope Psalm 23 works like my yard props and reminds you to rest. A practical application of this passage could be to start scheduling blocks of time to be still and alone with our strong Savior. I recommend literally putting "Jesus dates" on the calendar so we aren't tempted to schedule something else in His place.

I also think it's a good idea to find (or create) your very own figurative "green pasture." A place—perhaps a hammock, swing, chaise, or laundry room with soft piles to collapse in—where you feel totally comfortable reclining with God. Of course candles and chocolate might make your pasture even more comfy!

And finally I'd encourage you to take your strolls with the Good Shepherd in the morning because communing with Him starts off the day even better than a double cappuccino!

The right-now relevance of Psalm 23

God's love frees us from frenzied lives and compels us to rest—even those of us who aren't naturally inclined to recline!

ENOUGH ABOUT ME. WHAT ABOUT YOU?

1. Reread Psalm 23 slowly. What verse do you most identify with, and why?

2. Have you ever felt Jesus snatch you up by the neck when you were headed for the brink of disaster? If so, describe what being sternly rescued by the Good Shepherd felt like.

3. How would you grade yourself on the subject of real rest? Does learning to be quiet with God come naturally, or do you have to work at it?

4. Where is your current personal green pasture or still water? In other words, where do you go when you want to really connect with God?

5. Rewrite Isaiah 50:4–5 in your own words. What do you think it means to have ears that have been awakened? What can you do practically to improve your spiritual attention span?

6. Read John 6. What were the practical ramifications of Jesus's walking away from the crowd to be alone with His Father? In what situations do you think the "ends" of rest justify the "means" of disappointing people?

11

GOD DOESN'T STUTTER

How Psalm 119 sheds light on this supernatural love letter

called the Bible

—

The Lord's chief desire is to reveal himself to you
and, in order for him to do that,
he gives you abundant grace.
—MADAME JEANNE GUYON

M y friend Kim Hill and I often have the privilege of appearing together at women's conferences. She leads worship with her award-winning voice, and I get to tell stories about Jesus with my bottomless bucket of words! One of our goals for each conference is to make sure that every woman is prayed for specifically before she leaves. But since we don't want anyone to feel intimidated or embarrassed, we came up with the idea of passing out prayer-request cards midway through our events and telling women not to write their names but simply share their spiritual needs as honestly as possible, knowing their identities won't be exposed. Hostesses then gather up the cards to pass back out among the crowd at the end of the day for a time of nonthreatening intercessory prayer.

Kim and I first facilitated one of these intentionally anonymous seasons of prayer at a large event in Fort Lauderdale. After giving the women time to quietly contemplate and pray over the anonymous requests they'd been handed, we identified a few general concerns, such as marital problems or prodigal children, and asked anyone holding a prayer card dealing with those issues to stand up on behalf of the woman who wrote it. Then we spent several minutes praying out loud for God's will to be accomplished in the broken hearts and lives of the people each woman was blindly representing.

After we'd prayed the last prayer, sung the last song, hugged everyone within squeezing distance, and officially concluded the event, Kim went into the foyer to sign CDs. A woman approached her and declared, "I have to tell you about the prayer card I got. But first I need to tell you a little bit about my background." She described how she'd become addicted to cocaine and lost her marriage and custody of her children as a result. Then she got to the good part, where God reached down and rescued her from the pit of addiction and self-destruction. She told Kim about the divine healing she'd experienced through a twelve-step program and how God eventually restored her to her husband and kids. Then she handed Kim her prayer card and said, "Read this."

> What's the most recent "sovereign God moment" you've experienced—a situation where you knew what happened to you wasn't simply coincidence but could only be orchestrated by God Himself?

When Kim looked down, she scanned these words: "Please pray for me! I'm addicted to crack, and my life is falling apart. Last week my husband said he'd had enough, and he took our kids and left me. I don't know what to do." When Kim looked up, the redeemed prodigal said with a smile, "Now you tell me our God's not sovereign."

That extraordinary card exchange is one of my favorite stories from the road because it provides a tangible example of how God goes to great lengths to reveal Himself to desperate people. How He weaves single, seemingly unconnected threads into a gorgeous tapestry of grace. There's simply no way our team could've coordinated ferrying one specific prayer request to one particular woman, sitting among an audience of thousands, who'd experienced the exact same situation. Only an omnipotent God could accomplish that feat!

WONDERFUL WORDS OF LIFE

Psalm 119 is another tangible, even encyclopedic example of how God graciously reveals Himself to us. Next to its length (it's the longest of all 150 psalms), the most obvious feature is the way it's equally divided into twenty-two distinct stanzas. Plus each of these stanzas begins with a successive letter of the Hebrew alphabet, so this psalm is also a well-thought-out acrostic.[1]

In his book *Reflections on the Psalms,* C. S. Lewis contrasts the intentional layout of Psalm 119 with the more extemporaneous, emotional style of other psalms:

> This poem is not, and does not pretend to be, a sudden outpouring
> of the heart like, say, Psalm 18. It is a pattern, a thing done like
> embroidery, stitch by stitch, through long, quiet hours, for love of the
> subject and for the delight in leisurely, disciplined craftsmanship.[2]

How much must God love us to go to the trouble of disclosing Himself in such an exquisitely meticulous manner?

Now because of its heft, we can't ponder every line of Psalm 119 in this chapter, so we're going to focus on the first, twelfth, and last stanzas. And while perusing only three passages of this magnum opus is admittedly like reading the CliffsNotes of a Shakespearean play, they do loudly proclaim both the benefits of God's Word and the innate messiness of readers like us who get to reap those benefits. The psalmist begins by connecting personal happiness with obeying Scripture:

> Happy are those who live pure lives,
> who follow the LORD's teachings.

Happy are those who keep his rules,

    who try to obey him with their whole heart.

They don't do what is wrong;

    they follow his ways.

LORD, you gave your orders

    to be obeyed completely.

I wish I were more loyal

    in obeying your demands.

Then I would not be ashamed

    when I study your commands.

When I learned that your laws are fair,

    I praised you with an honest heart.

I will obey your demands,

    so please don't ever leave me. *Psalm 119:1–8, NCV*

In my early twenties I worked for a youth ministry organization where, to save money, the staff members shared in the janitorial duties. We took turns cleaning the entire office once a week. Since I preferred hanging out with kids and talking about Jesus over cleaning toilets, I wasn't as thorough as I should've been in my early days on staff. One morning the head secretary confronted me with furrowed brows and an overflowing trash can and said, "Your style of cleaning is just a lick and a promise, a lick and a promise!" I could tell she was frustrated, but I'd never heard that saying before. When I asked my boss what it meant, he laughed and explained, "She's trying to tell you that you're not putting very much energy or effort into the job!"

Unfortunately, people of faith tend to approach the Bible with a lick and a promise too. We're more likely to read a book about God than to ponder the life-giving words He breathed. Believe it or not, this isn't a consequence of our fast-paced modern lives either. Back in the eighteenth century, German theologian Martin Boos put it this way: "Most read their Bibles like cows that stand in the thick grass, and trample under their feet the finest flowers and herbs."[3] I'm not sure which is worse: being accused of having a crummy work ethic or being compared to a cow! Nevertheless, like the psalmist, I sincerely want to be more loyal about studying and obeying God's Word. Because in addition to the side dish of happiness promised in Psalm 119:1, Jesus proclaims Scripture has the

> **PSALMS:**
> **THE INSIDE STORY**
> Psalm 119 is formally classified as an orphan psalm because the identity of its author is unknown.

power to sustain us more than literal food (see Matthew 4:4). And as a self-appointed gourmand, I'm intrigued by anything that's touted as being better than tasty cuisine!

THE LIMITLESSNESS OF GOD'S LAW

Leapfrogging to the beginning of the twelfth stanza (essentially the mid-way point) of Psalm 119, we find our unidentified songwriter continuing the theme of venerating Scripture. But he turns his attention from the benefits we receive from reading the Bible to the infinite perfection of the Book itself:

> LORD, your word is everlasting;
>> it continues forever in heaven.
> Your loyalty will go on and on;
>> you made the earth, and it still stands.
> All things continue to this day because of your laws,
>> because all things serve you.
> *Psalm 119:89–91, NCV*

My stepfather held the office of superintendent of schools when I was little and therefore had to give a lot of speeches. I beamed proudly whenever I got to hear him, because he was a gifted orator. Everyone in the audience seemed to lean forward when John vigorously approached the microphone, because he had such an incredible command of the English language.

Of course, around the house he didn't pontificate like a politician; he spoke in a way I could understand. I can remember sitting at the dinner table long after the plates had been cleared, listening wide-eyed while John captivated us with stories about the good ol' days or about his dangerous exploits in the navy during World War II. Growing up, I pricked my ears at pretty much anything that fell out of John Angel's mouth. That's one of the reasons it's so sad watching him struggle to find words now in the wake of Alzheimer's.

The way my stepfather tailored his speech to his audience brings to mind John Calvin's seminal thesis about Christianity, the *Institutes,* in which he wrote a famous passage about God "lisping":

> For who even of slight intelligence does not understand that as nurses commonly do with infants, God is wont in a measure to "lisp" in speaking to us? Thus such forms of speaking do not so much express clearly what God is like as accommodate the knowledge of him to our slight capacity. To do this he must descend far beneath his loftiness.[4]

But we must not misconstrue Calvin's assertion to mean that God stutters or that His inscripturated words are somehow less than perfect. Calvin wasn't describing the Bible as inferior; he was describing us as inferior! God never struggles to find the right words like my weakening stepfather; His "lisping" is compassionate condescension so as to communicate in a way humans can understand.

It's incredibly humbling to consider the Creator of the universe "dumbing Himself down" so we can read His thoughts. God's Word is

---

PSALMS: THE INSIDE STORY

Eight synonyms for *Scripture* are used in the 176 verses of Psalm 119. Translated into English from the original Hebrew text, in order of appearance, they are: *law, testimonies, precepts, statutes, commandments, ordinances, word,* and *promise.*[5] In light of this keen emphasis on Scripture, some detractors have accused the author of Psalm 119 of worshiping the Word. However, if you read this psalm carefully, you'll notice his praise is actually directed toward God, the Author of Scripture!

---

flawless…limitless…timeless. Yet He breathed it with mercy because He knew messy readers like us needed to understand it.

IMAGINE THE BIBLE IN A RED BATHING SUIT

The latter part of Psalm 119's twelfth stanza describes God's Word as a lifesaver:

> If I had not loved your teachings,
>> I would have died from my sufferings.
> I will never forget your orders,
>> because you have given me life by them.
> I am yours. Save me.
>> I want to obey your orders.

Wicked people are waiting to destroy me,
>   but I will think about your rules.
Everything I see has its limits,
>   but your commands have none. *Psalm 119:92–96, NCV*

Every spring and summer throughout high school and most of college, I worked as a lifeguard. When I wasn't patrolling the beach at Lake Swan Camp, I was corralling slippery kids at Sanford Bath and Tennis Club or overseeing sunburned tourists at Wekiwa Springs State Park. However, for all the days spent twirling a whistle around my finger while wearing a red bathing suit, I don't think I ever truly saved anyone's life.

Oh, I had lots of so-called rescues, but they usually consisted of pulling a panicky dog-paddler out of the deep end or assisting a fatigued swimmer who only thought he couldn't make it back to shore. There was one close call when I rushed toward the screams of an exceptionally large, fear-stricken woman wedged in an inner tube. But I heroically responded with a few well-aimed squirts of body oil, and out she popped, crisis averted.

> **JUST A CONVERSATION PIECE?**
>
> Ninety-three percent of Americans say they own at least one copy of the Bible,[6] but 41 percent say they rarely or never read the Bible.[7] Only half of the adults interviewed nationwide could name at least one of the four gospels.[8]

In contrast to my ho-hum lifeguarding career, when the psalmist exclaims, "I will never forget your orders, because you have given me life by them" (verse 93 NCV), he's not implying the Bible is standing around looking bored and hoping we will get in over our heads so it can jump in and cool off. Nor is God's Word simply a raft to flop on when we get a little winded. Scripture isn't a lifeguard; it's a lifesaver. Without its guidance, we would surely be swept away by the undertow of our own bad choices, faulty reasoning, and prejudiced decisions. Left to our own devices, we would all get hopelessly stuck in some kind of situational inner tube. If we don't cling to the promises in this love letter written to us by our heavenly Father, the peace and joy in our hearts will sputter and flail and eventually sink to the bottom. We simply can't swim successfully in the sea of life without God's counsel.

THE TEACHER'S PETS ARE MESSY

Seventy-three verses later we come to the last stanza of Psalm 119, likely scribbled on parchment just as the psalmist's pen was running out of ink!

> Hear my cry to you, LORD.
>> Let your word help me understand.
> Listen to my prayer;
>> save me as you promised.
> Let me speak your praise,
>> because you have taught me your demands.
> Let me sing about your promises,
>> because all your commands are fair.
> Give me your helping hand,
>> because I have chosen your commands.
> I want you to save me, LORD.
>> I love your teachings.
> Let me live so I can praise you,
>> and let your laws help me.
> I have wandered like a lost sheep.
>> Look for your servant, because I have not forgotten your
>> commands. *Psalm 119:169–176, NCV*

Retired English pastor Michael Wilcock, a distinguished commentator on the psalms, describes this last section of Psalm 119 as a prayer with two requests: *Lord, hear* and *Lord, act.*[9] This sounded awfully whiny to me at first, like a child tugging at his mother's skirt pleading, "Listen to me, Mommy! Help me, Mommy!" Then I remembered what Jesus says about children:

> "Truly, I say to you, whoever does not receive the kingdom of God like a child shall not enter it." And he took them in his arms and blessed them, laying his hands on them. *Mark 10:15–16*

This is one of my favorite scenes in the New Testament. In my modern-context mind, I picture Jesus and the disciples at the mall. Most of them head off to Sears to look at camping equipment because their sleeping bags are lumpy and their tattered tents need mending. Only Jesus and Pete are left standing in the food court. They're both contemplating the Chick-fil-A menu (my imagination always defaults to Chick-fil-A in this musing because they're a Christian-owned company!) when a little boy who's sitting with several other rowdy children yells, "Hey, look, guys. That's the Lamb of God over there!" His buddies turn to see what he's pointing at. Then before their mothers have a chance to grab them, they all leap to their feet and race across the french-fry-littered linoleum toward Jesus.

But Peter stops them before they reach their target. He steps away from the Chick-fil-A line, placing himself between these enthusiastic kids and Immanuel. He gives them an admonishing stare and says, "What do you think you're doing, approaching the Messiah like that? Look at you. You've got apple pie on your shirts and chocolate shake smeared all over your faces. Go get your mamas to take you to the rest room and get cleaned up. When you come back, form a single-file line, and then I'll let you meet Jesus. But no touching, understand?" As those precious, yet deflated, pumpkins start to turn away, Jesus puts an arm around His indignant disciple's shoulders and says, "Aw, Pete, let 'em pass. I love sticky kids!"

While Psalm 119 does end with a childlike plea for God's help, His Word also reveals that He adores children. Throughout Scripture, stories similar to this one highlight God's perfect love for imperfect people and assure even the messiest of us that we can draw close to our Creator. So how about picking up a Bible and crawling into your Redeemer's lap?

THE PICK OF THE LITERARY LITTER

It's amazing to consider that the Bible gathering dust on our shelves is the same book preteen Jesus was teaching to a group of wide-eyed adults when Joseph and Mary accidentally returned home from the temple without Him (see Luke 2:41–50); it's also what the Good Shepherd held in His hand when a bunch of judgmental jerks threw at His feet a trembling woman they'd trapped in their adultery sting operation (see John 8:1–11). Philip Yancey says it best when he describes the Old Testament: "These are the prayers Jesus prayed, the poems he memorized, the songs he sang, the bedtime stories he heard as a child, the prophecies he pondered."[10]

Furthermore, because of God's favor, we live in the age of Old *and* New Testaments. Which means the progressive revelation in our Bibles includes the life and ministry of Jesus. It's packed full of fantastic stories about His healing lepers and hugging little ones! So why in the world are we more likely to pick up a *People* magazine or to covetously scan the pages of the latest Pottery Barn catalog? My goal is to go easy on the literary brain candy of our culture and spend more time perusing the supernatural words our heavenly Father spoke.

Wouldn't it be great to be able to earnestly exclaim like the psalmist?

Oh, how I love all you've revealed;

I reverently ponder it all the day long....

Your words are so choice, so tasty;

I prefer them to the best home cooking.

Psalm 119:97, 103, MSG

⤚ *The right-now relevance of Psalm 119* ⤙

God's love frees us from stumbling around on our own, giving us practical, lifesaving guidance and a clearer perspective on our circumstances through His Word.

ENOUGH ABOUT ME. WHAT ABOUT YOU?

1. If you could walk in the sandals of one character from the Bible for a week, who would it be, and why?

2. Why do you think modern believers and seekers tend to be bored with traditional Bible studies?

3. If you were to plan a nontraditional Bible study, describe some of the main components. For example, where would you meet? What would the schedule entail? Would it be

interactive, like a book club, or more lecture oriented, like a classroom?

4. Read all the way through Psalm 119 in one sitting. How would you distill the overall theme of this chapter into one sentence?

5. Which verse in particular resonates with you with regard to good times, and which do you identify with the most with regard to bad times?

6. Read James 1:22–25. While you were reading Psalm 119, what did the Holy Spirit prompt you to do?

12

STOP WATCHING YOUR FEET; JUST DANCE

What Psalms 149 and 150 suggest about

how rhythm-challenged people like us

can master the smooth moves of praise

The most valuable thing the Psalms do
for me is to express the same delight in God
which made David dance.
—C. S. Lewis

Most women I meet at retreats and conferences around the country are wonderful; I typically walk away thinking, *Wow, if I lived in this town, I'd definitely hang out with those girls!* But every now and then I'm invited to speak at an event populated with stiff and stodgy chicks. And those occasions feel like plowing concrete. Perhaps you've had a similar experience at a church gathering or PTA meeting where you felt as if you'd walked onto the set of *The Stepford Wives* and were the only woman still in possession of a genuine personality.

At one such event several years ago, I meandered around during the reception before the formal program started, trying to find someone to talk to. As I was mentally lamenting the lack of friendliness, someone introduced me to the retreat worship leader, who was also a guest at the gathering. Thinking we might be able to bond as aliens and strangers in "Stiffville," I initiated a conversation with her. I mentioned how much I loved music and confessed that her part of the program was usually my favorite. Then in an effort to connect, I said with a wink, "You'd better keep an eye on me during the up-tempo songs, because I might just break out into a worship dance."

Please believe me when I say I was only kidding. Although Scripture and church history feature many beautiful, God-honoring precedents of worship dancing, I was raised as a Baptist. In my experience *boogie* and

Baptist are oxymoronic terms! But of course the worship leader had no way of knowing this. Have you ever attempted to joke with someone you didn't know well and realized he or she didn't get your humor? Well, I could tell by this woman's contemplative facial expression that she thought I was serious. But before I had a chance to amend my verbal gaffe and explain that I was just being silly, the evening program began.

Of course I planned to clarify my comments later, but the following morning was hectic, and I didn't have a chance to chat with the worship leader prior to the opening session. When Wanda gave me a conspiratorial grin while mounting the stairs to lead worship from the stage, my stomach relocated itself in my throat. She sat down at their old upright piano and enthusiastically belted out the first song in her set. When we finished singing the last stanza, Wanda smiled down at me and then confided to the group, "Ladies, I have such a treat for you this morning!" After pausing dramatically she proclaimed, "Lisa is a *worship dancer*!"

Much to my horror she descended the stairs and presented me with a giant purple and gold flag—replete with glittering symbols for *Alpha* and *Omega*. After a quick thumbs-up she trotted back to the piano and started playing an upbeat anthem, with a nod toward me as if we'd rehearsed a routine. For one moment I stood there like a deer in the halogen headlights of a particularly large car, thinking, *Surely they're playing a joke on me, because this is like some humiliating clip from* Candid Camera. My second thought was, *Oh well, they probably won't invite me back here anyway!* And I started to twirl.

> What were you feeling the last time you danced in public?

Although I'm usually more of a private dancer—I prefer my living room to formal sanctuaries—I sincerely believe wiggling is good for the soul. Whether we're bopping to a literal beat or swaying to an internal song, dancing can be a very beneficial endeavor. Especially when we're gyrating because of God! It's easy to get distracted by the doldrums of life or else to be frozen with anxiety about what other people think of us, but when we keep God at the very center of our hearts and minds, His grace is like one of those big, sparkly disco balls; it will inspire us to pirouette with praise!

SUNDAY MORNING FEVER

One of my favorite chapters in King David's life is when the Israelites finally brought home to Jerusalem the Ark of the Covenant, the ceremonial box that held tangible relics representing God's faithfulness throughout Jewish history.[1] The manly monarch was so happy he developed a serious case of "Saturday night fever":

> The people told David, "The LORD has blessed the family of
> Obed-Edom and all that belongs to him, because the Ark of God
> is there." So David went and brought it up from Obed-Edom's
> house to Jerusalem with joy. When the men carrying the Ark of
> the LORD had walked six steps, David sacrificed a bull and a fat
> calf. Then David danced with all his might before the LORD. He
> had on a holy linen vest. David and all the Israelites shouted with
> joy and blew the trumpets as they brought the Ark of the LORD to
> the city. *2 Samuel 6:12–15, NCV*

According to the narrative at the beginning of 2 Samuel 6, this is actually the second time David tried to bring the ark back to Jerusalem. Unfortunately his first crack at recovering the ark ended in disaster, because in their haste David and his buddies ignored some of God's rules. So during this subsequent attempt, they were especially careful to do everything right. It was probably a slow, quiet march as everyone focused on the Old Testament regulations of appropriate ark transportation. But

when the Levites toting the supernatural package finally started hiking up
the hill toward the center of Jerusalem, David couldn't control his delight
and started dancing!

> David, ceremonially dressed in priest's linen, danced with great
> abandon before GOD. *2 Samuel 6:14, MSG*

In light of this *Dancing with the Stars*–style display by the author of
nearly half of the psalms, it's fitting that the last two entries in the ancient
hymnal include exhortations to dance:

> Praise the LORD!
>
> Sing a new song to the LORD;
>> sing his praise in the meeting of his people.
>
> Let the Israelites be happy because of God, their Maker.
>> Let the people of Jerusalem rejoice because of their King.
> They should praise him with dancing.
>> They should sing praises to him with tambourines and
>>> harps.
> The LORD is pleased with his people;
>> he saves the humble.
> Let those who worship him rejoice in his glory.
>> Let them sing for joy even in bed!
>> *Psalm 149:1–5, NCV*

In addition to the "bebop blessing," I also like how this second-to-last
psalm encourages God's people to sing a *new* song. It's not okay for us to
plod into the Lord's presence with listless lyrics. It's not acceptable for us

to recite liturgy or hum familiar melodies like automatons. Worshiping our Redeemer shouldn't resemble being on the assembly line at some widget factory.

Remember that old infomercial from the nineties with the blond diet guru who yelled, "Stop the insanity!" in an attempt to inspire chubby couch potatoes across America? Well, maybe it's time for someone to stand up and yell, "Stop the staleness!" in churches across the country.

PSALMS: THE INSIDE STORY

The last five psalms (Psalms 146–150) are often referred to as the hallelujah psalms. Most Old Testament scholars agree these five psalms correspond to the five thematic "books" within the Psalter.[2]

A general synopsis of the five books within Psalms is
- Psalms 1–41 = Book 1, which covers the proclamation of the covenant and David's conflict with Saul;
- Psalms 42–72 = Book 2, which covers David's reign as the second king of Israel;
- Psalms 73–89 = Book 3, which covers the Assyrian crisis;
- Psalms 90–106 = Book 4, which covers the destruction of the temple in Jerusalem and the period of Babylonian exile;
- Psalms 107–150 = Book 5, which covers Israel's postexilic period.[3]

Because, honestly, how can Christians be dull and disengaged when God's grace is so amazing that He sacrificed His only Son to rescue us? The miracle of our salvation should inspire fresh music and at least a little toe tapping!

WARNING: GRATITUDE MAY CAUSE GYRATIONS

My friend Kim had an aha moment about wholehearted rejoicing while leading worship at a women's retreat a few months ago. One side of the room was full of conventional Christians who sang along in harmony with suitable clapping, while the other side was filled with women from a charismatic congregation who were much more demonstrative. They clapped enthusiastically, swayed to the rhythm of the music, and sometimes shouted things like "Glory to God!" or "Thank You, Jesus!" between songs.

Kim was fine with their animated worship, but some of the other women weren't. One of them cornered her during a break to say that, since it was a multidenominational event and inclusive of all worship styles, she believed the other women's effusive praise was inappropriate. She complained that she and her friends felt uncomfortable and asked Kim to tell the other participants to tone it down.

Kim reluctantly approached the leader of the exuberant girls and explained the situation. The woman's face fell with disappointment, but she graciously agreed to ask "her side" to temper their zeal. Then she told Kim if only the others knew what God had rescued them from—drug addiction, physical abuse, paralyzing shame from abortions, and more—perhaps they'd be more tolerant of her crew's enthusiasm.

Kim said her heart broke during the first song of the next set because those precious women who'd been so full of life now seemed deflated. Their earnest enthusiasm was replaced with undeserved disgrace. Propriety had trumped passion. So Kim stopped strumming her guitar and started speaking her mind. She expressed regret for asking anyone to rein in her ardor for God. She lamented the way Christians tend to value decorum more than delighting ourselves in the Lord. She touched on the point made by the women's ministry leader, that if we knew what others had been saved from, we'd be more compassionate and less critical. By the time she was through, the traditional team wanted to wiggle during worship too!

Kim's experience reminds me of the story about a woman who washed Jesus's feet with her tears, dried them with her hair, and then anointed them with expensive perfume (see Luke 7:36–50). Religious people misinterpreted her behavior as improper. But Jesus justified her extravagance when He proclaimed, "She was forgiven many, many sins, and so she is very, very grateful" (verse 47, MSG).

The jubilant praise described in Psalm 149 isn't just for Pentecostals or teenagers or Promise Keepers eating hot dogs and cheering in a football stadium. It's a biblical template for all believers to express how we're very, very grateful for God's affection and forgiveness!

GOOD FOR THE MIND AS WELL AS THE SPIRIT

As if we needed more incentive to kick up our heels in praise, a study of the elderly published in the *New England Journal of Medicine* found that those who dance three to four times a week "showed 76 percent less incidence of dementia" than those who boogie less often or not at all.[4]

FANCY FOOTWORK AND FIGHTING EVIL

Remember *Footloose*, the 1984 movie that made Kevin Bacon a star? Although the language was at times less than edifying, everyone (except for maybe a few grumps) walked out of the theater smiling after that feel-good flick. The surface story is about how a brash metropolitan boy, Ren McCormack (portrayed by Bacon), who loves dancing and loud music finds himself relocated to a small, conservative Midwestern town where those things are strictly forbidden. So boom box in hand, Ren sets out to transform the stiff local culture.

The movie's tag line is "He's a big-city kid in a small town. They said he'd never win. He knew he had to." Which alludes to the film's deeper story line. In spite of cheesy dialogue and cutesy dance numbers, *Footloose* is about fighting injustice, prejudice, and hypocrisy. It's about confronting obstacles that stand in the way of what's right. It's about one "good guy" going up against an entrenched regime of "bad guys." (In this case the bad guys are led by a rule-enforcing preacher, who recognizes his mistakes and becomes a good guy again before the credits roll.)

The last three verses of Psalm 149 remind me of the movie *Footloose* because, while the context of this psalm is about dancing, it includes a part about fighting for what's right. In other words, God's sock hop includes a routine with swordplay:

> Let them shout his praise
>   with their two-edged swords in their hands.
> They will punish the nations
>   and defeat the people.
> They will put those kings in chains
>   and those important men in iron bands.
> They will punish them as God has written.
>   God is honored by all who worship him.

> Praise the LORD! *Psalm 149:6–9, NCV*

Where Psalm 149:6–9 departs significantly from the *Footloose* movie metaphor is that we don't fight the battle of good versus evil alone. The divine war we're enlisted in as Christians (see also 2 Corinthians 10:3–6 and Ephesians 6:10–18) doesn't consist of one plucky young soldier facing a battalion of bad guys by himself. On the contrary, we march into battle behind our Messiah, the King of kings. Jesus leads the charge against the forces of evil in our world. Plus, we've got proof that *He will win the war* (see Revelation 19:11–21). We aren't twirling in worship while wielding a sword because we're being flippant about the fight; we can dance because we already know who wins!

SAVE THE LAST DANCE FOR HIM

The Psalter ends with an exhortation for God's people to worship Him with abandon. We're directed to fill heaven and earth with praise, to play exuberant tunes on a virtual symphony of instruments, and, of course, to dance:

> Praise the LORD!
>
> Praise God in his Temple;
>> praise him in his mighty heaven.
> Praise him for his strength;
>> praise him for his greatness.
> Praise him with trumpet blasts;
>> praise him with harps and lyres.
> Praise him with tambourines and dancing;
>> praise him with stringed instruments and flutes.
> Praise him with loud cymbals;
>> praise him with crashing cymbals.
> Let everything that breathes praise the LORD.
>
> Praise the LORD! *Psalm 150, NCV*

It's interesting that Psalm 1 was essentially a tutorial about holy behavior, while this last one is an invitation to boogie. The beginning of the Psalter expounds on our responsibilities, and the finale reminds us to rejoice. Which is fitting, because in light of everything the ancient hymn writers explore in these 150 songs—feasts and famines, joy and sorrow, life and death, friends and foes—God's loving presence is unmistakable throughout. Regardless of how difficult and disheartening life got, these Old Testament musicians knew that God was sovereign and full of compassion, that everything ultimately would work out for their good and His glory.

And let's not forget, the psalmists were looking forward to Jesus. They believed God's promises but didn't get to experience a flesh-and-blood Messiah. We live on the "Christmas and Easter really happened" side of progressive revelation. We *know* Jesus came to this earth in the form of a baby boy. We *know* He lived a perfect, sinless life. We *know* after thirty-something years He walked up a hill and stretched out His arms to be nailed onto a tree. We can hold in our own hands historical accounts of how Jesus sacrificed His life so we could be reconciled with our Redeemer. Therefore, we have an even greater reason to celebrate than the psalmists had!

Just Remember to Let Him Lead

A few weeks ago I was speaking at a conservative church's retreat where wiggling during worship wasn't encouraged (the constrained atmosphere there was not unlike that of the fictional town in *Footloose*). But for some reason I felt compelled to teach on Psalms 149 and 150 during the last session. I explained that, while there aren't any directives in Scripture to wear hose, there are several directives exhorting God's people to dance—to praise Him with abandon.

Afterward a soft-spoken woman approached to say she was pleasantly surprised that I had brought up the topic of dancing in Scripture. She went on to explain how a few days before the retreat she sensed God whispering, *I want you to learn to dance with Me,* during her devotional time. She continued sheepishly, "Because I'm black, people assume I have good rhythm, but I've actually never been much of a dancer. I've always been more serious minded than free spirited. So when God asked me to dance, I initially felt very self-conscious and awkward." Then she smiled and said, "But when you started talking about dancing this morning, I clearly heard God whisper again. This time He told me to stop watching my feet and look at His face."

And therein lies the secret for closeted Christian dancers everywhere: *Don't worry about your footwork; just look at God and let Him lead.* Whether we are literally engaged in boogie fever or simply enjoying a mental samba, dancing with God involves our souls more than our soles. It means leaning into God's faithfulness—trusting that because of grace He sees in us the perfect partner—and then starting to twirl.

When David recognized the compassion in God's countenance, he rejoiced. He didn't care if the people watching thought he was crazy. He didn't mind if they thought his spiritual soft-shoe wasn't suitable behavior for a king. He didn't even pay attention to the cease-and-desist glare from his wife, Michal.[5] He praised God because, much like the inevitable spray that results when you shake a soda can and then pull the tab, he simply couldn't suppress his gratitude for God's grace.

That's how those of us who delight in the Lord must live. Because of God's *great* love for us—revealed through His Word and realized through Jesus—we will dance, at least in the ballrooms of our hearts.

⟿ *The right-now relevance of Psalms 149 and 150* ⟿

God's love frees us from worrying about our lack of rhythm and polish so we can dance with abandon in praise of His goodness.

ENOUGH ABOUT ME. WHAT ABOUT YOU?

1. In what ways do you typically express complete joy if nobody's looking? How is that different from when you have an audience?

2. Since the psalms are full of directives to "sing for joy" (5:11; 67:4), "clap your hands" (47:1), "lift up your hands in the sanctuary" (134:2, NIV), and "praise his name with dancing" (149:3), what does that imply for Christians whose personal style tends to be less demonstrative?

3. How does God's Spirit usually rouse your soul from rote worship? Describe a few situations when you've been appropriately stretched in private or corporate worship.

4. Read Psalm 30:11. Describe a specific season when God unexpectedly transformed your sorrow into celebration.

5. Would you describe your relationship with Jesus in the terms of a fast dance, like a fox trot or a samba, or a slower number, like a waltz? Explain why.

6. Reread Psalm 150. Old Testament scholar Derek Kidner describes how this concluding psalm answers the "where, why, how, and who" questions regarding praising God.[6] How would you answer those questions after perusing it?

7. Of the thirteen psalms we've examined in this book, which one is your favorite right now? Why?

ONE FINAL THOUGHT

Thank you so much for sampling these choice psalms from God's Old Testament buffet bar with me. I trust your heart has been encouraged as we've savored the supernatural hope they contain.

I truly believe we'll be able to warble "I love your teachings," like the psalmist sings in Psalm 119:174 (NCV), when we begin to understand how relevant Scripture really is. How the historical narratives and poems and parables and epistles that flowed from our heavenly Father's mouth through the pens of ancient writers still apply to every facet of our daily existence.

How on the morning we get that dreaded phone call to find out someone we love just passed away, we can open our Bible and regain a sense of peace and perspective:

But let me reveal to you a wonderful secret. We will not all die, but we will all be transformed! It will happen in a moment, in the blink of an eye, when the last trumpet is blown. For when the trumpet sounds, those who have died will be raised to live forever. And we who are living will also be transformed. For our dying bodies must be transformed into bodies that will never die; our mortal bodies must be transformed into immortal bodies.

Then, when our dying bodies have been transformed into bodies that will never die, this Scripture will be fulfilled:

"Death is swallowed up in victory.
O death, where is your victory?
   O death, where is your sting?"
      1 Corinthians 15:51–55, NLT

How during moments of delight, when we can't seem to stop our laughter from overtaking our sense of propriety, we can find a giggling soul mate in Proverbs 31:

Strength and dignity are her clothing,
   and she laughs at the time to come. *verse 25*

And during sleepless nights when we can't stop fretting about something shameful in our past, we will find comfort when we flip to the far right of God's Word and read:

If we confess our sins, he is faithful and just and will forgive us our sins and purify us from all unrighteousness. *1 John 1:9, NIV*

Following a pleasant rain shower this morning, I went out and picked fifteen ripe raspberries from my garden. After baptizing them in the kitchen sink, I popped them in my mouth and meandered out to check on the grapevines winding up a backyard pergola. I was delighted by how many new bunches of grapes had appeared since my last inspection a week or so ago. Then I tiptoed over to a bird's nest huddled in the low rafters of the porch roof to play Peeping Tom with a darling gang of baby robins. Finally I strode up the hill toward the deck to look at how some new plants were doing—and almost stepped on a big black snake slithering through the wet grass!

I jumped over him with a yelp and then leaped onto the deck. I was so rattled I had to stand there for a few minutes to catch my breath and regain my composure. I really hate snakes! Along with roaches and smarmy men wearing pinkie rings and excessive cologne, they are the bane of my existence. And that's not the first beady-eyed monster I've come across in my rural Tennessee Eden either. I've already spotted two in the yard this year, and another actually had the audacity to crawl into my house through a fireplace on a scorching hot day last summer. Suffice it to say that little sucker didn't make it home for dinner in one piece!

While I can't stand creepy crawlers, I've come to accept that they're part of the bargain of living in the country. I don't have to deal with traffic jams or nosy neighbors, but I have to coexist with all kinds of critters. My backyard juxtaposition of beauty and beast reminds me that life includes good and bad; thankfully, our Redeemer is sovereign in both. His grace abounds from fresh berries and Technicolor sunsets to scaly creatures and cellulite! His Word is so perfectly comprehensive it speaks to *every* single aspect of our often messy existence.

Now to him who is able to keep you from stumbling
and to present you blameless before the presence of his glory with great joy,
to the only God, our Savior, through Jesus Christ our Lord,
be glory, majesty, dominion, and authority,
before all time and now and forever. Amen.
Jude 24–25

NOTES

Introduction

1. John Calvin, *Commentary on the Book of Psalms* (Grand Rapids: Eerdmans, 1949), 1:xxxvii.

Chapter 1

The epigraph to this chapter is taken from Eugene H. Peterson, *Answering God: The Psalms as Tools for Prayer* (San Francisco: Harper & Row, 1989), 25.

1. Norm Geisler and Ted Cabal, eds., *The Apologetics Study Bible* (Nashville: B&H, 2007), 789.

2. Spiros Zodhiates, ed., *Hebrew-Greek Key Word Study Bible* (Chattanooga, TN: AMG, 1996), 627, 1911.

3. Michael Steger, "How to Be Happy," *New Scientist,* March 22, 2008, www .newscientist.com/article/mg19726485.000-comment-how-to-be-happy.html.

4. John MacArthur, ed., *The MacArthur Study Bible* (Nashville: Word, 1997), 743.

5. See 1 Kings 5:1–11.

6. Geisler and Cabal, *The Apologetics Study Bible,* 789.

7. Tremper Longman III, *How to Read the Psalms* (Downer's Grove, IL: InterVarsity, 1988), 45.

Chapter 2

The epigraph to this chapter is taken from Martin Luther, *What Martin Says.*

1. Tremper Longman III, *How to Read the Psalms* (Downer's Grove, IL: InterVarsity, 1988), 24.

2. V. Phillips Long, "Psalms and Wisdom Literature" (class lecture and syllabus notes, Covenant Seminary, St. Louis, Missouri, September 13– December 6, 2004).

3. Edwin Robertson, *Dietrich Bonhoeffer's Meditations on Psalms* (Grand Rapids: Zondervan, 2002), 28–29.

4. Emily Thornwell, *The Lady's Guide to Perfect Gentility* (New York: Derby and Jackson, 1856), 87.

5. Herman Ridderbos, *Paul: An Outline of His Theology* (Grand Rapids: Eerdmans, 1975), 253–58.

6. See 2 Samuel 15–18.

7. Spiros Zodhiates, ed., *Hebrew-Greek Key Word Study Bible* (Chattanooga, TN: AMG, 1996), 2023.

Chapter 3

The epigraph to this chapter is taken from Marva J. Dawn, *My Soul Waits: Solace for the Lonely in the Psalms* (Downer's Grove, IL: InterVarsity, 1983), 175.

1. Michael Wilcock, *The Message of Psalms 73–150* (Downer's Grove, IL: InterVarsity, 2001), 260.

2. John Gray, "The World of Hair," www.pg.com/science/haircare/hair_twh_5.htm.

3. Spiros Zodhiates, ed., *Hebrew-Greek Key Word Study Bible* (Chattanooga, TN: AMG, 1996), 1957; and *NLT Study Bible* (Carol Stream, IL: Tyndale, 2008), 1019.

Chapter 4

The epigraph to this chapter is taken from Richard Foster, *Prayer: Finding the Heart's True Home* (New York: HarperCollins, 1992), 31.

1. C. S. Lewis, *The Problem of Pain* (San Francisco: HarperCollins, 1940), 122.

2. See 1 Corinthians 6:19–20.

3. See Genesis 2:25–3:13.

4. See Leviticus 14:6; Numbers 19:16–19.

5. Lesslie Newbigin, *The Gospel in a Pluralistic Society* (Grand Rapids: Eerdmans, 1989), 222.

6. Neal Krause and Christopher G. Ellison, "Forgiveness by God, Forgiveness of Others, and Psychological Well-Being Late in Life," *Journal for the Scientific Study of Religion* 42, no. 1 (March 2003): 77–93.

7. Michael Card, *A Sacred Sorrow* (Colorado Springs, CO: NavPress, 2005), 21.

8. Card, *A Sacred Sorrow,* 21.

9. Derek Kidner, *An Introduction and Commentary: Psalms 1–72* (Downer's Grove, IL: InterVarsity, 1973), 193–94.

Chapter 5

The epigraph to this chapter is taken from Charles Haddon Spurgeon, "Owl or Eagle?" Metropolitan Tabernacle Pulpit, March 10, 1872, www.spurgeongems.org, sermon no. 2860.

1. See Exodus 2:11–3:1.

2. See 1 Kings 18–19:4.

3. See Exodus 3:2–22.

4. See 1 Kings 19:5–18.

5. See 1 Chronicles 6:16, 22, 31–48; 2 Chronicles 20:19.

6. Derek Kidner, *An Introduction and Commentary: Psalms 1–72* (Downer's Grove, IL: InterVarsity, 1973), 165.

7. Victor Parachin, "Fears About Tears? Why Crying Is Good for You," *Vibrant Life,* November–December 1992, http://findarticles.com/p/articles/mi_m0826/is_/ai_12930434.

8. Arnold Dallimore, *Spurgeon: A New Biography* (Edinburgh, UK: Banner of Truth, 1987), 186.

9. See Job 16:16; Psalm 6:6–8; Lamentations 2:11; Luke 19:41–42.

Chapter 6

The epigraph to this chapter is taken from Elie Wiesel, *Night* (New York: Hill and Wang, 1958), 118. This quote came from a later translation of

Night, copyright 2006, which includes Elie Wiesel's Nobel Peace Prize acceptance speech of 1986, copyrighted by the Nobel Foundation.

1. See Exodus 11:8; Nehemiah 5:6.

2. *Webster's Encyclopedic Unabridged Dictionary of the English Language* (San Diego, CA: Thunder Bay, 2001), s.v. "imprecate."

3. See 1 Chronicles 16:4–5.

4. See Joshua 9:1–2; Judges 3:28–30; Joshua 13:1–7.

5. See Judges 7.

6. Walter Kaiser and others, *Hard Sayings of the Bible* (Downer's Grove, IL: InterVarsity, 1996), 280.

7. See Judges 4–5.

8. Tremper Longman III, *How to Read the Psalms* (Downer's Grove, IL: InterVarsity, 1988), 138–40.

9. Wiesel, *Night,* viii.

Chapter 7

The epigraph to this chapter is taken from Brennan Manning, *A Glimpse of Jesus: The Stranger to Self-Hatred* (New York: HarperCollins, 2003), 45.

1. Charles Haddon Spurgeon, *The Treasury of David* (Grand Rapids: Kregel, 1976), 478.

2. Gerard Van Groningen, *Messianic Revelation in the Old Testament* (Eugene, OR: Wipf and Stock, 1997), 1:390.

3. Tremper Longman III, *How to Read the Psalms* (Downer's Grove, IL: InterVarsity, 1988), 67–68.

4. Derek Kidner, *An Introduction and Commentary: Psalms 73–150* (Downer's Grove, IL: InterVarsity, 1973), 395.

5. See 1 Samuel 17.

6. See Judges 7.

7. Westminster Abbey, "Queen Elizabeth II's Coronation in the Abbey—2 June 1953," www.westminster-abbey.org/search/11465.

8. Wikipedia, "State Opening of Parliament," http://en.wikipedia.org/wiki/State_Opening_of_Parliament.

Chapter 8

The epigraph to this chapter is taken from Martin Luther King Jr., *Letter from Birmingham Jail,* quoted in Os Guinness, *The Call* (Nashville: W Publishing, 2003), 73.

1. Derek Kidner, *An Introduction and Commentary: Psalms 1–72* (Downer's Grove, IL: InterVarsity, 1973), 65.

2. Michael Wilcock, *The Message of Psalms 1–72* (Downer's Grove, IL: InterVarsity, 2001), 40.

3. Blaise Pascal, *Pensées* (New York: Dutton, 1958), 58.

Chapter 9

The epigraph to this chapter is taken from Philip Yancey, *The Bible Jesus Read* (Grand Rapids: Zondervan, 1999), 127.

1. Derek Kidner, *An Introduction and Commentary: Psalms 1–72* (Downer's Grove, IL: InterVarsity, 1973), 138.

2. Kidner, *Psalms 1–72,* 139.

3. *Canonical* means "relating to or belonging to the biblical canon," that is, the list of books established as genuine and complete Holy Scriptures.

4. See 1 Samuel 21:10–22:2.

5. See 1 Samuel 21:9.

6. John MacArthur, ed., *The MacArthur Study Bible* (Nashville: Word, 1997), 411.

7. Robert A. Emmons and Michael E. McCullough, "Highlights from the Research Project on Gratitude and Thankfulness," http://psychology.ucdavis.edu/labs/emmons/.

Chapter 10

The epigraph to this chapter is taken from Tim Hansel, *When I Relax I Feel Guilty* (Colorado Springs: David C. Cook, 1979), 22.

1. See 1 Samuel 16:11–13.

2. See 1 Samuel 17:34–37.

3. Charlotte A. Schoenborn and Patricia F. Adams, "Sleep Duration as a Correlate of Smoking, Alcohol Use, Leisure-Time Physical Inactivity, and Obesity Among Adults: United States, 2004–2006," Centers for Disease Control and Prevention, National Center for Health Statistics, May 2008, www.cdc.gov/ nchs/products/pubs/pubd/hestats/sleep04-06/sleep04-06.htm.

4. Peter Craigie and Marvin Tate, *Word Biblical Commentary, Psalms 1–50* (Nashville: Thomas Nelson, 2004), 207.

5. Marva J. Dawn, *My Soul Waits: Solace for the Lonely in the Psalms* (Downer's Grove, IL: InterVarsity, 1983), 262.

6. Dawn, *My Soul Waits,* 263.

7. Derek Kidner, *An Introduction and Commentary: Psalms 1–72* (Downer's Grove, IL: InterVarsity, 1973), 112.

8. See 2 Samuel 9.

9. Kidner, *Psalms 1–72,* 112.

Chapter 11

The epigraph to this chapter is taken from Madame Jeanne Guyon, *A Short and Easy Method of Prayer,* quoted in Richard Foster, *Devotional Classics* (New York: HarperCollins, 1990), 323.

1. See also "Psalms: The Inside Story" in chapter 9.

2. C. S. Lewis, *Reflections on the Psalms* (San Diego: Harcourt, 1958), 58–59.

3. Quoted in Charles Haddon Spurgeon, *The Treasury of David* (Grand Rapids: Kregel, 1976), 510.

4. John Calvin, *Institutes of the Christian Religion,* 1:13:1.

5. Derek Kidner, *An Introduction and Commentary: Psalms 73–150* (Downer's Grove, IL: InterVarsity, 1973), 417–19.

6. Jennifer Robison, "The Word on Bible-Buying," Gallup, June 18, 2002, www.gallup.com/poll/6217/Word-BibleBuying.aspx.

7. Alec Gallup and Wendy W. Simmons, "Six in Ten Americans Read Bible at Least Occasionally," Gallup, October 20, 2000, www.gallup.com/poll/2416/Six-Ten-Americans-Read-Bible-Least-Occasionally.aspx.

8. George Gallup Jr., *The Role of the Bible in American Society* (Princeton: Princeton Religion Research Center, 1990), 17.

9. Michael Wilcock, *The Message of Psalms 73–150* (Downer's Grove, IL: InterVarsity, 2001), 218.

10. Philip Yancey, *The Bible Jesus Read* (Grand Rapids: Zondervan, 1999), 25.

Chapter 12

The epigraph to this chapter is taken from C. S. Lewis, *Reflections on the Psalms* (San Diego: Harcourt, 1958), 45.

1. See Exodus 25:10 22.

2. Eugene H. Peterson, *Answering God: The Psalms as Tools for Prayer* (San Francisco: Harper & Row, 1989), 125–28.

3. V. Phillips Long, "Psalms and Wisdom Literature" (class lecture and syllabus notes, Covenant Seminary, St. Louis, Missouri, September 13–December 6, 2004).

4. "Dance Away Dementia," *Natural Life*, January–February 2004, 22, www.naturallifemagazine.com/0402/JanFeb04.pdf.

5. See 1 Chronicles 15:29.

6. Derek Kidner, *An Introduction and Commentary: Psalms 73–150* (Downer's Grove, IL: InterVarsity, 1973), 490–92.

ABOUT THE AUTHOR

Rarely are the terms *hilarious storyteller* and *theological scholar* used in the same sentence, much less used to describe the same person, but then, Lisa Harper is anything but stereotypical. She has been lauded as a gifted communicator whose writing and speaking memorably connect the dots between the Bible era and modern life.

Best-selling author and pastor Max Lucado calls Lisa one of the "best Bible tour guides around," and speaker Priscilla Evans Shirer adds, "If anyone can help us to hear, understand, and receive the truth of Scripture, it is Lisa Harper."

Her vocational résumé includes six years as the director of Focus on the Family's national women's ministry, where she created the popular Renewing the Heart conferences, followed by six years as the women's ministry director at a large church in Nashville. Her academic résumé includes a Master of Theological Studies with honors from Covenant Seminary in St. Louis.

Now a sought-after Bible teacher and speaker, Lisa has spoken at many large multidenominational events, such as Women of Faith and Moody Bible and Focus on the Family conferences. She's appeared on numerous syndicated radio and television programs and is a regular columnist for *Today's Christian Woman*.

In spite of her credentials, the most noticeable thing about Lisa is her authenticity. When asked about her accomplishments, she responded, "I'm definitely grateful for the opportunities God's given me; but don't forget, He often uses donkeys and rocks!"

You can contact Lisa at
www.lisaharper.net

Exceptional Event Opportunities for 2009-10!

A Night of
REAL *Christmas*

COMING
Clean

A Night of Real Christmas and **Coming Clean** are two unique
inspirational events featuring Grammy-nominated artist Kim Hill and
author and Bible teacher Lisa Harper. Both women are known for their
humor, depth, and authenticity; their engaging style guarantees a program
that will encourage everyone!

A Night of Real Christmas promises a special evening when women in
your community will be transformed by the miracle that took place in a
manger. Through worship, story, and biblical exposition, **Coming Clean**
invites women into a transparent relationship with Jesus so they can truly
flourish in God's incomparable affection. These events can be tailored to fit
both ladies' night out and retreat settings.

For more information on booking either of these events
for your church or ministry, please visit
www.lisaharper.net or www.kimhillmusic.com.